The brick book

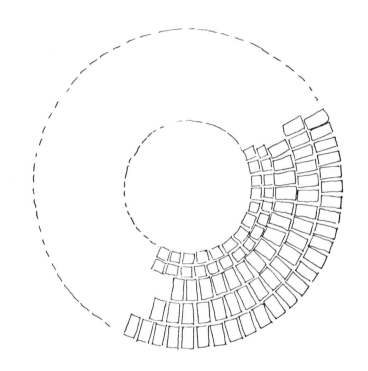

The brick book

The unique how-to-build-it book full of imaginative ideas and practical projects in brick—from a beginner's barbecue to a summer house.

Robert Hayward

Thomas Y. Crowell Company
Established 1834   New York

Produced by Walter Parrish International Limited, London
Manufactured in the United States of America

Library of Congress Cataloging in Publication Data

Hayward, Robert
  The brick book.
  Includes index.
  1. Building, Brick—Amateurs' manuals.
  2. Bricklaying—Amateurs' manuals. I. Title.
  TH 1301. H39   693.2'1   77-22
  ISBN   0-690-01448-1

*Page 6: A brick-faced fireplace can break up large areas
of plain with soft textures and clean lines.*

*Page 8: Simple brick arch and niche gives this small
porch a sunny, Mediterranean feel.*

To J and J

My thanks are due to the following people who have helped me with the preparation of this book: John Holden for his advice; Philip Griffiths for help with the drawings; Walter Ritchie for advice on brick sculpture and above all my editor, Heather Jones, for her infinite patience and encouragement.

Contents

Introduction

It is a wonderful feeling to look at something you have built with your own hands—all the days of hard work are soon forgotten, even though the final result may not be quite what you would expect from the professionals. Never mind, half the fun is doing it yourself. But there is no fun in embarking on something which is totally beyond you. Obviously some people have a greater degree of skill than others and this book caters for a wide range of skills. The first part provides you with the basic knowledge you need for any general straightforward brick-laying work. The second part consists of specially designed projects each shown in an artist's sketch. Many of them are simple; it will be sufficient to read the introductory pages—how to lay bricks, cut them, make foundations, mix mortar, concrete, which tools to use etc. to be equipped with the skills you need to accomplish them. But the larger projects, the Garden room and Summer house in particular, demand a lot of planning and preparation and must not be attempted by anyone who has not already attained a substantial degree of skill in construction work. If you decide to build them you will have to plan the work carefully, first of all clearing permission for the building with any relevant authority. You will also have to make sure that the excavation does not interfere with any main services to the house such as gas or electricity. The building work itself, where large columns and roof beams are involved, will necessitate the use of portable scaffold towers and pulleys. These can usually be hired on a daily rental basis but don't forget that this will add to the cost of the project.

All building materials are expensive these days, so before you do any buying, get estimates from several suppliers. It is most important that you cost each project carefully and thoroughly before you start. Make sure that you can buy further stocks of the same materials from the same supplier in case you need them and do not underestimate the time it will take to build even one of the smaller projects;

during this period of time you will have to store all the materials in a place secure from harsh weather and this could be a major problem, if you do not give it careful consideration before you begin. For costing purposes, use the materials list given at the beginning of each project. In some cases you will have to use the list as a basis for calculating what you need for your particular situation—the Fireplace and Shelves are examples of this as the actual quantities required will depend entirely on individual wall heights, lengths etc. In these cases we have given dimensions for a 'typical' situation but you will have to calculate actual numbers of bricks, quantities of mortar and other materials from our guidelines and from the estimating tables at the back of the book. These tables should also be used to work out amounts of bricks, mortar and concrete required for any bricklaying you wish to do apart from the projects.

Also, for those projects that involve casting a concrete slab, you will need wooden forms to hold the concrete while it sets. We have not felt it necessary to specify this in the materials lists since, for large areas, it is probably best to hire forms from a specialist contractor, once again on a daily rental basis. This will also be a consideration when you are costing the project.

In the text we have given all dimensions in imperial and metric units—imperial first and metric equivalents in brackets, but in the drawings, where space was at a premium, we have given only imperial units except in cases where the text does not give the required dimensions. We have used centimetres and metres throughout, although in Great Britain it is common practice in the building industry to specify sizes in millimetres—however this is a peculiarity and the conversion from centimetres to millimetres is a simple one. All timber (lumber) sizes are given as nominal standard sawn sizes.

We have recommended throughout that you use

a standard size brick. We mean by this the standard size in your particular country, since there is in fact no international 'standard' size although the same idea is followed in all countries: the length of a standard-sized brick is approximately twice its depth and this results in an easily manageable unit.

On the whole we have given *general* instructions regarding such building procedures as how deep foundations should be dug, the thickness of footings and the need for damp-proof courses in walls. These procedures are actually determined by regional factors like weather patterns, soil composition and so on, and in countries with vastly differing climatic zones, there are strict building codes which have been drawn up with these factors in mind. In the United States, for example, foundations even for low garden walls should always be below the frostline—the line below which frost does not penetrate and disturb the soil. The frostline varies quite dramatically across the country—from an inch below the surface in southern Texas to six feet in Northern Maine. It is important to know what the rules are in your area. Your building code is designed to stop you making errors and it should always be consulted before a large project is undertaken.

Local considerations also govern bricks themselves and in particular the availability of certain types of brick. Some special shapes like the bullnose brick which we have specified for some of the projects, as a design feature, might be difficult to obtain or prohibitively expensive in some areas. If you find this to be the case, you could adapt the project and substitute ordinary regular bricks, resulting in only a slight change in the appearance of the finished design. All the projects have been designed so that they can be adapted fairly easily and they can be used as a source of ideas. For instance, if you wish, you can apply the Summer house beam-and-column structure to a pergola or use one niche of the pergola on its own for shady seating area. There are many such variations possible with the versatile brick which can give you tremendous satisfaction so long as you build wisely and within your own capabilities. If you experience any problems at all, don't let pride stand in the way of safety, seek advice from the experts.

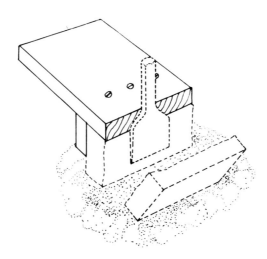

Bricks and brickwork

A short history

Bricks have been used for shelter and protection for many thousands of years; so long, in fact, that the word 'brick' has come to suggest solidity and permanence. The long-lasting popularity of bricks is due, in some degree, to the ease with which they can be handled by the bricklayer who can hold a brick in one hand and pick up mortar on a trowel with the other; he can also follow his plans with a facility which other materials do not allow. Probably for these reasons, the basic size of a brick remained virtually unchanged for many hundreds of years. Whether you are in the U.S., Britain or Australia, it is interesting to know something of the long worldwide tradition behind today's brick buildings.

Essentially, the story of brick building is the story of finding a good brick-making earth in places where there is a lack of other building materials, like wood and stone. In Holland and many parts of North Germany, where there is a shortage of these two, brick has traditionally been used for every kind of building. In other parts of the world, in the United States for instance, brick has been used for both attractive appearance and enduring quality; it often appears as a 'veneer' on wood-frame houses and has always had a certain prestige value.

Today, most bricks are machine-made in highly automated factories. While mass-market builders can achieve the effects they desire with mass-produced bricks, the individual builder may still search for hand-made bricks, slightly irregular, full of texture and variety—a pleasant survival from the days when bricks were made in small local yards where the earth was dug and fired in the same small area.

Even despite modern technical achievements, the process of producing a brick is still basically the same as it has been for the last 10,000 years—bricks are still shaped blocks of baked earth.

Left: Seventeenth-century brickmaking in Holland—J Luiken, Trades and Professions, *Amsterdam, 1694.*

Right: Early 19th-century bricklayer at work—from The Saturday Magazine, *1836.*

The first bricks were unfired; they were shaped crudely by hand and left out in the sun to bake. Unfired bricks are still used in many parts of the world even today. In Anatolia, Turkey, for instance, and in some parts of Russia, many crude dwellings are made of unfired earth: the Mexican word 'adobe' is taken from the Spanish and literally means 'mud'. Although unfired bricks have a considerable crushing strength, the mud brick has the distinct disadvantage of being washed away in the rain: after a particularly heavy rainfall the walls have to be replastered with fresh earth.

Sun-dried bricks are so effective, however, that even though early Neolithic man was familiar with the effect of high temperature on clay for making his pottery, he did not apply it to brick-making until quite late (3rd millennium BC). There are some specimens dating from this period from the Indus Valley in the Museum of Ancient Brick in Johnson City, Tennessee.

Around this same period, in the Middle East although bricks were still sun-dried, the innovation of a box mould to facilitate their manufacture was introduced: the celebrated walls of Jericho begun at the beginning of the 3rd millennium BC were made in this way. The soil around this area, being malleable and plastic, lent itself perfectly to brick-making and did not require the use of a binding medium like straw, which was the method in Egypt. Evidence of very early mud bricks has been found all over the Middle East, Central and South America, Turkey and India.

By 600 BC, in Babylon and the Sumerian cities of present day Iran, some beautiful decorative work was achieved with fired and glazed bricks. Vast palace complexes were embellished with processions of archers, lions, bulls and winged beasts.

It was the Romans who first introduced bricks into Britain where the climate demanded the durability of burnt bricks, although at home the Romans were using both burnt and sun-dried bricks—the latter probably being more common. The Roman brick was thick and squarish, like a tile. They were used for small structures like houses and shops and for bonding courses in the flint or rubble walls of their forts and garrison towns in south-east England. In the 1st and 2nd centuries AD Roman brickwork was technically and aesthetically at its best, with regular mortar joints

Left: Detail of decorative brickwork on a minaret at Gulpaygan, Iran c. 1100.

Above: Persian glazed-brick relief of a winged beast from the Palace of Darius at Susa, c. 500 BC.

made one half-width of the brick itself, giving a pleasing, neat appearance. In the 4th and 5th centuries, bricks of different colours began to be used as patterning on buildings. Brick-making in England ceased when the Roman legions left in 410 and thereafter Roman bricks served for many centuries as secondhand material, recovered from previous building and used in the construction of Norman and Saxon buildings. It was not until the advent of the mediaeval great brick, rough in texture and red in colour, that bricks were again commonly made in Britain.

On the Continent of Europe brick-making did not cease when the Roman legions left and bricks were used, especially in the Low Countries and North Germany, to build fine majestic cathedrals in the Gothic style. This fashion on the Continent for impressive brick building had a great influence in England but it was not really until the Tudor period that the wealthy were eager to substitute elaborate decorative brickwork for stone and wood. And without a doubt, it was the reign of Henry VIII that saw the great age of English brick. Hampton Court Palace majestically confirmed the fashion, employing bricks on a massive scale. Elaborate Tudor chimneys, gigantic and eccentric, began to spring up all over London and in many country areas—a rich contrast to the usually plain brick fabric of the rest of the building. Brick was now used in towns and countrysides for houses, palaces, institutional buildings and churches.

The fashion for brick building has continued in England up to the present day, surviving even the brick taxes of the 18th century.

Above: Moulded brickwork on early Tudor manor house. East Barsham Manor, Norfolk, England.

Left: Imposing Tudor chimney stacks at Hampton Court Palace, Middlesex, England c. 1520.

Right: Rippled brick pattern—a common mechanically textured brick.

Today, all over the United States, there are magnificent examples of the American version of the English Tudor house with lots of brick often combined with wood—the style that began in the 1500s in England has lasted, with modifications, until the heyday of the American suburb.

Although wood and stone have been the most common building materials in America, the brick-built house has always signified taste and style and in areas like Pennsylvania, even though wood and stone are in plentiful supply, brick has always been used in preference to either of these.

The brick industry in the U.S. reached its peak just before and after World War I; some of the first sky-scrapers, although steel-framed, were clad in solid and massive brickwork but for this type of building, brick was soon superseded by concrete.

It's true to say that brick-faced homes remain a perennial favourite—their warmth and texture blend with everything from bronze-glass skylights to simple painted porches. Even in the busy cities, small brick buildings add charm and a human scale to our land- and city-scape.

TYPE OF BRICK

There is a vast range of colours, textures, sizes and strengths of brick available. The exact classification of bricks is a specialist field and here we can only give the barest bones of the story, but as you will be buying bricks on a comparatively small scale, this will be enough. Most of the terms used in this book are used on both sides of the Atlantic; any unfamiliar ones can be found in the glossary at the back.

There are two basic varieties of clay bricks:
Common or building bricks. These have no claim to an attractive appearance so tend to be cheaper than other bricks. They are made for general building work and where appearance is unimportant, below ground, for instance. This is not an indication of quality and common bricks can have high strength and weathering values.

Facings or face bricks. As their name implies, these bricks are made to give an attractive appearance and are available in a wide range of strengths, colours and textures. They come in red, blue, purple, yellow, brown and grey, varying in depth of colour, and also as certain mixtures, e.g. multi-red. The colour depends on the type of clay and the firing process. They can also be smooth, sandfaced (where sand is incorporated into the face of the clay) or mechanically textured. Many of this type of brick are not really suitable for conditions of special exposure to exceptionally harsh frosty weather.

Quality

In America common and facing bricks are graded according to national specifications into three categories: Severe Weathering (SW), Moderate Weathering (MW) and Negligible Weathering (NW). For areas with severe climate variations, especially where bricks will be exposed to heavy rain and frost and come in contact with the ground (as with retaining walls), you should use SW bricks (generally today the most readily available type of brick). Where moderate resistance to weather is required use MW. NW should only be used as back-up for interior masonry where the brickwork will not be subject to freezing and thawing.

In Britain, the British Standard has the categories Internal, Ordinary and Special to distinguish bricks suitable only, in the first case, for internal work, in the second case, for normal exposure, and in the third, for extreme exposure conditions. One type of brick called an 'engineering' brick generally attains this last quality. These bricks are fired at a very high temperature and because of this they absorb little moisture and have a high crushing strength. Some facings and commons are suitable for extreme exposure, but do not assume this unless it is specified by the manufacturers.

Shape

Facing bricks are also available in special shapes including splayed or rounded edges. In some of the projects we will be using bullnose bricks, plinth stretchers and single cant facings which fall into this category (see opposite).

Manufacturing methods

Bricks can also be referred to by the process by which they are made.

Hand-made. These bricks are expensive; they are made by hand in moulds. They look really good because of their natural texture and slightly irregular shape but cost a lot more than their

Below: Rough-textured brick used by Saarinen at Philadephia University.

Opposite above: A selection of specially shaped bricks, some with cores, including two bullnose headers (top, extreme left and right); two single-cant bricks (below the bullnoses); a plinth header (bottom row, second from left) and an extra-long plinth stretcher, (bottom row, centre).

Opposite below: Frogged bricks.

machine-made cousins. They can be ideal for small jobs where appearance is most important.

Machine-made. Most bricks are made by machine today. There are several processes and on the whole they do not affect us. As a matter of interest, however, the main ones are:

Soft-mud—a high moisture content clay is used and the process is really an adaptation of the handmaking method.

Wire-cut—a process whereby a column of clay comes out of the machine and the bricks are cut off by wires resulting in a brick of even shape and size.

Bricks are often made with perforations or indentations such as the 'frog'. This is generally a device for reducing weight. The frog is useful in providing a key for the mortar in wall-building, so remember always to let it face upwards. In pavings, however, it should not be placed face upwards but sideways, or downwards if you are laying on a sand bed. Bricks with perforations, called cored bricks, are more common in the U.S.

Calcium silicate bricks

All the bricks we have described so far have been clay bricks, but there is another kind of brick which is made from a mixture of hydrated lime and sand or crushed stone or a mixture of both. They are called calcium silicate bricks.

These bricks may be tinted during the manufacturing process but their natural colour is 'off-white'. They are particularly suitable for internal use; they look good but are not suitable for every purpose so we will not be recommending their use in most instances.

Size

There are dozens of different sizes of bricks available in most countries today. The U.S. in particular offers a huge variety; bricks ranging in thickness from $3''$ to $8''$, in height from $2''$ to $8''$ and in lengths up to $16''$ can be bought. Except for such universal names as 'standard', 'Roman' and 'Norman', the name of bricks denoting their sizes often varies from manufacturer to manufacturer, so it is always advisable to specify the type of brick you want by dimensions rather than name.

In the U.S., except for the non-modular 'standard', 'oversize' and $3''$ units, most bricks are produced in 'modular' sizes. The nominal dimensions of a 'modular brick' are equal to the manufactured dimensions plus the thickness of the mortar joint for which the unit is designed. In general, joint thicknesses are either $\frac{3}{8}''$ or $\frac{1}{2}''$ and so if you wish to use a $\frac{1}{2}''$ mortar joint, let's say, the dimensions of the brick you will buy will be very slightly smaller than if you wish to use a $\frac{3}{8}''$ mortar joint. We recommend throughout this book that, for a neat appearance, you use a $\frac{3}{8}''$ mortar joint. We have included in the back of the book a table showing several common brick sizes available in the U.S. with their manufactured and nominal dimensions.

There are some sizes of bricks in the U.S. including the standard modular (nominal dimension: $4'' \times 2\frac{2}{3}'' \times 8''$) and the SCR brick (nominal dimension: $6'' \times 2\frac{2}{3}'' \times 12''$) which are designed so that the height of the bricks including mortar is a standard $2\frac{2}{3}''$, thus giving three vertical courses to $8''$. These would be easy sizes to work with for all projects in this book but if you wish to use bricks with a different height, consult the vertical coursing table at the back which will tell you how high your brickwork should be rising vertically in feet and inches for a given number of courses.

Even coursing is essential for good brick-laying and must be checked constantly as you are building. In our specifications for projects, where the height of any brickwork is critical, we have given measurements in feet and inches (or metric units) in order that you can calculate your correct number of courses.

In the U.K. there are not so many different brick sizes and the one most commonly used is the standard $4\frac{1}{8}'' \times 2\frac{5}{8}'' \times 8\frac{5}{8}''$. These dimensions may seem rather strange but in fact when used with a $\frac{3}{8}''$ mortar joint they conveniently result in multiples of $3''$ (height) and $9''$ (length), giving a vertical basis for calculation of four courses to $1'$. The metric brick which is now common in the U.K. is very slightly different in size from the imperial brick and measures $215\text{mm} \times 102.5\text{mm} \times 65\text{mm}$ and this, used with a 10mm joint, gives a modular size of $225\text{mm} \times 112.5\text{mm} \times 75\text{mm}$.

Basically it does not matter what size of brick you use, so long as you adjust the number of courses you need to reach a desired height in feet and inches. We do, however, recommend you use a brick whose bed depth dimension is approximately half its length so that the bonding will work correctly (see p. 37). This is true for length as well, since, no matter what the length of a brick you have chosen you can adjust as necessary either by adapting the length of the wall you are building, or adjusting the number of bricks or by cutting bricks (some brick-cutting is always necessary in brick-work).

Because of the large number of different sizes available in most countries, we have somewhat arbitrarily chosen the standard size $4\frac{1}{8}'' \times 2\frac{5}{8}'' \times 8\frac{5}{8}''$ to work with throughout this book, but where dimensions are critical as, for instance, in building up columns, measurements are always given in feet and inches or in metric units, so you can always work out the exact number of bricks yourself, on the basis of the brick size you are actually using.

BUYING BRICKS

Check prices of bricks from various suppliers before you decide to buy from one in particular. The number of bricks and amount of mortar you will need will depend upon the pattern you use for your wall, patio etc. and the dimensions. Make sure that the supplier has a stock of bricks of the type you are using in case you want a further supply. Before you approach a supplier, it may be as well to consult the Brick Development Association in Britain or the Brick Insitute of America in the U.S., or equivalent, about your particular requirements and they will direct you to a suitable manufacturer. When you order your bricks from a supplier, ask about delivery charges. It's a good idea to pay a little more to have the bricks delivered on a pallet instead of having them just dumped on the ground and many of them broken.

APPEARANCE

Anyone building a brick wall instinctively avoids placing one joint above another by overlapping the bricks. The overlapping is known as bonding and contributes both to the strength of the wall and its appearance. The dimensions of a standard brick conveniently allow the builder to build in a pattern to his brickwork as the bonding proceeds. Bricks are referred to structurally according to their positioning in the wall. A brick used lengthways is a 'stretcher' and a brick used across the

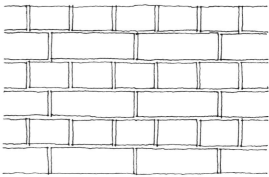

English bond

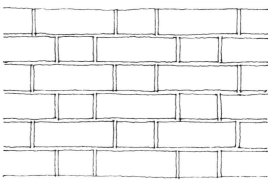

Flemish bond

Stretcher (running) bond

width of the wall is a 'header'. Because, in standard brick sizes, a header is just about half the width of a stretcher, a jig-saw arrangement of headers and stretchers can be built up which can give the wall great strength as well as resulting in attractive patterns which, especially from a distance, have a

Above: Strong geometric patterning adds visual interest to this elegant early-16th-century house —'The Vyne', Hampshire, England.

Right: Strong patterning results from mortar joints of contrasting colours used as decoration on this wall of a school in St John's Wood, London.

certain eye appeal.

The most common bonding arrangements are traditionally known as: English bond, Flemish bond, and stretcher (running) bond; these terms are also used in the United States.

The bonding pattern can be given a further dimension if a different-coloured brick is used for some of the headers to produce a strong geometrical design like, for instance, the diaper patterns so popular in the 15th and 16th centuries.

There are unending varieties of decoration that can be produced with a little practice but one of the most important aspects is to make sure any additional brickwork will co-exist harmoniously with what is already there.

MORTAR

We have discussed types of bricks, colours and textures and bonding patterns: another important element in the appearance and strength of a brick wall is the type of mortar which fills the joint between bricks. We discuss mixing mortar and finishing off the mortar joint (called jointing or tooling) on pages 26 and 38. Mortar is made from cement, lime and sand in various proportions, but the basic ingredients of the mortar mix can be varied to produce different colours. The final colour of the brickwork depends to a surprising degree upon the colour and detail of the joints, particularly when viewed from a distance. It can be used as a device to create large-scale patterns and to emphasize certain parts of the wall.

Tools and materials

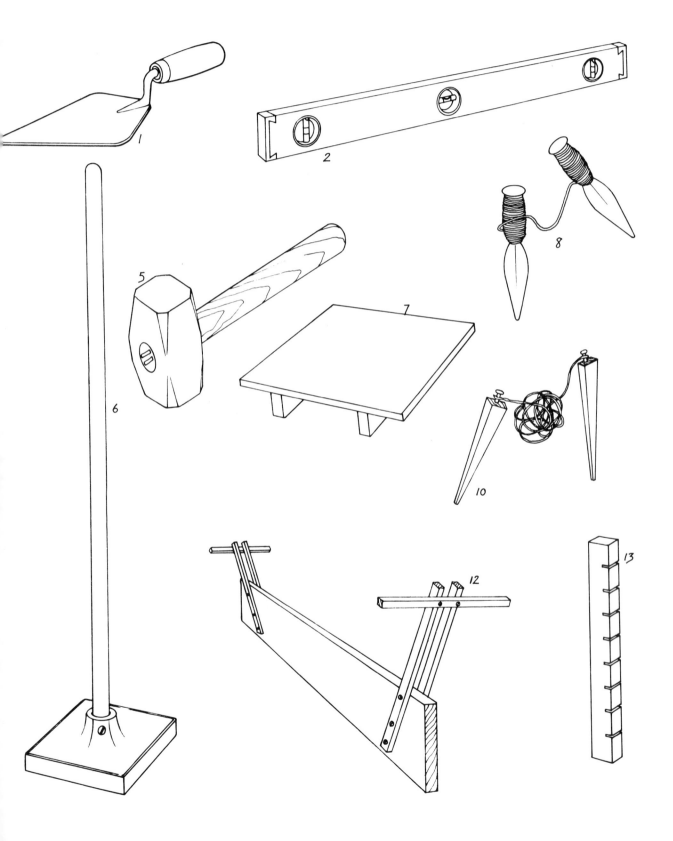

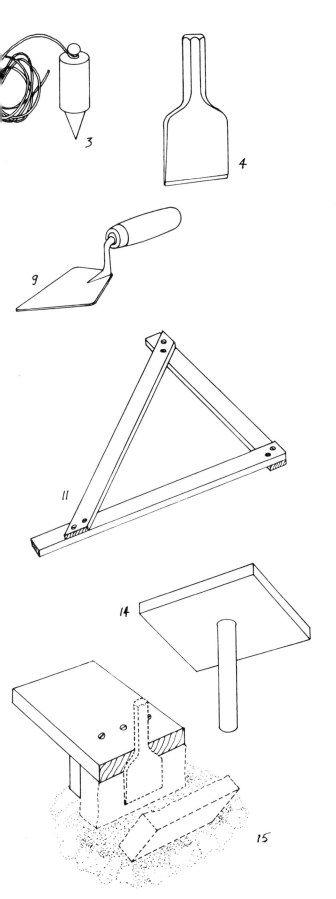

You will find that many of the tools needed will already be in your workshop—hammers and saw for making forms for steps, or spades for digging foundations—but there are some more specialized tools that are essential for getting professional results in bricklaying and you should borrow or buy all of these, or in some cases make them yourself.

Basic tools

1 Pointed trowel with a 10″ (25cm) blade for 'buttering' bricks with mortar.

2 A 2′ (60cm) spirit level with two types of bubbles to check horizontal and vertical plane.

3 Plumb bob to check a wall's vertical plane.

4 Broad-bladed chisel (brick set or bolster) for cutting bricks

5 Broad-faced hammer for cutting bricks.

6 Rammer for compacting soil.

7 Spotboard for mixing mortar. Make it from plywood 2′ (60cm) square, raised on bricks.

Special tools

8 Line and pins (or long nails) for building up even courses.

9 Pointing trowel.

10 Short stakes and cord. These are used for 'laying out' lines and angles.

11 Right-angle square. Make this as a large triangle of 1″ × 2″ (2.5cm × 5cm) wood with sides in the proportion of 3:4:5. (Remember, the angle opposite the longest side will be the right-angle.)

12 Tamping board for compacting and levelling concrete. This will have to be made 'on the spot' depending on your width of concrete.

13 Gauge rod for making sure brick walls rise at the correct rate. Make it of 1″ × 2″ (2.5cm × 5cm) wood marked with saw cuts. If you are using British standard bricks make these cuts every 3″ to ensure that your brickwork rises four courses to 1′ and if you are using American standard bricks mark it every $2\frac{2}{3}$″ to ensure three courses to 8″. For non-standard American sizes consult the vertical coursing table at the back of the book.

14 Hawk for holding small amounts of mortar as you point your brickwork. Make it from 9″ (23cm) square plywood screwed to a short piece of broom handle.

15 Bat and closer gauge. The bonding pattern of your wall may call for the frequent cutting of half bricks (half bats) or half bricks cut lengthways (queen closers) and this will be much easier if you make a gauge to the necessary width so you don't have to keep measuring the bricks each time before cutting—just slip the brick underneath and cut. This can also be adapted for mitre-cutting bricks (see page 55).

MIXING MORTAR

Mortar is made by mixing together Portland cement, lime and sand in varying proportions.

Below ground it should consist of one part cement to three parts sharp sand (no lime). We refer to this as 1:3 (volume, not weight). Above ground one part lime may be added to improve workability and the mix will vary according to the type of facing brick. A general all-purpose mix is one part cement, one part lime, six parts clean sharp sand (1:1:6). Mortar which is too strong in cement will not make the wall stronger; on the contrary, it can cause severe cracking. The mortar should always be slightly weaker than the brick as it will then absorb any small movements in the wall without cracking the bricks themselves.

It is best to make a spotboard for mixing mortar; this is a 2′ (60cm) square board raised clear of the ground (see page 25).

Mix the mortar in small amounts—as much at one time as you will use in an hour. Any mortar which has begun to set must be discarded; cement sets by chemical reaction, it doesn't dry, so you can't just add more water and re-mix. Mix the ingredients dry and then add water a little at a time. To test the consistency, take a handful of the mixed mortar and squeeze. It should be sufficiently plastic to hold the impression of the fingers.

The colour of the mortar can be varied easily by using coloured Portland cement. Colours include black, buff, chocolate, green and red.

Take great care that the quantities that go into the mix are correct as you can easily spoil the appearance of the wall. It is probably best to buy a prepared coloured mix. Although it can be expensive, it will be consistent in colour.

For the best effect use a mortar which is slightly lighter than, or of similar colour to, the brick. Strongly contrasting joints can be unattractive.

CUTTING A BRICK

Some brick-cutting is inevitable whether you are building walls or laying paths. You may be laying a herringbone pattern with an edging on a patio or a bond pattern for a wall which requires lots of 'half bats' or 'queen closers' (see page 37). Facility in brick-cutting comes with practice and a few wasted bricks can't be avoided at first.

The best tool for the job is the broad-faced chisel (bolster or brick set). Put the brick on a cushion of flat sand and mark with a wax crayon along the line to be cut. Place the chisel along this mark with the bevel facing away from the end to be used. Tap the brick gently to cut a groove across the two faces then strike firmly with the broad-faced hammer to sever.

If you really fail dismally at cutting bricks in this traditional manner, one solution is to hire a brick saw—a handsaw with hardened teeth set into a blade which simply saws the bricks across; or you can make a $\frac{1}{2}″$ (1.2cm) cut all round with the saw before using chisel and hammer.

Also recently available in 'do-it-yourself' stores is a wire brick-cutter; this has a ring handle each end of a wire with a cutting surface.

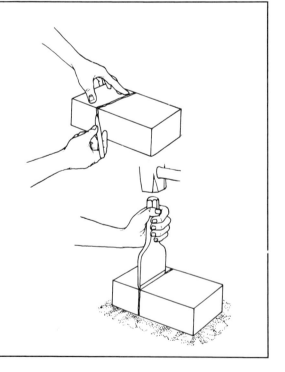

MIXING CONCRETE

For any work requiring a solid base or foundation, concrete is the material to use. It can be made quite simply by mixing together cement, aggregates (sharp sand and gravel) and water.

Cement comes in large paper sacks which are awkward to handle, so if you can get friends and neighbours to help, so much the better. For general purposes the concrete should be 1:2:4 mix by volume, that is, one part cement, two parts clean, sharp sand and four parts gravel. You can buy the sand and gravel already mixed as 'all-in aggregate' and, if you prefer this, the mix will be 1:6 with the cement. You can also buy ready-mixed dry cement and aggregates from a building supplier; you just add water. This is convenient but expensive.

It is important to store your cement and aggregates in a suitable place: make sure it is dry and that the aggregates are kept clean. Store them on boards or a metal sheet.

Measure the aggregates onto a piece of board or metal sheeting 6′ (2m) or so square, and measure the cement on top. Mix until the colour is even all through. Make a hole in the middle of the pile and add the water gradually, using a sprinkler on the end of a garden watering-can to prevent the small particles of cement being washed away. Shovel the dry mixture on

top. Do not get the mix too wet: it should be of a fairly stiff consistency. Rule of thumb: turn the whole mixture over ten times dry and ten times wet.

There are several alternatives to mixing by hand. For example, a small mixing-machine can be hired quite cheaply; the same proportions of cement and aggregates should be used but less water. The water could be poured in directly with a garden hose but be

careful not to add too much! If you have a large area to cover, it may be worthwhile getting a delivery of ready-mixed concrete brought straight to your site. This will arrive by special truck and can be poured into your foundation trench or wherever you wish.

Hints

1 Don't mix more concrete than can be laid in twenty minutes.
2 Don't mix concrete in the rain.
3 Don't lay concrete if the temperature is less than 34°F. (1°C).
4 Cover your concrete with tarpaulin while it is drying if there is any chance of frost or if the weather is hot and dry.
See page 180 for a simple table showing quantities of ingredients.

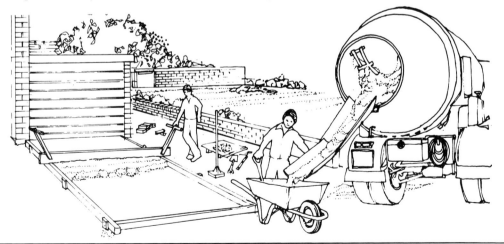

Walls

The purpose of a wall in a garden is essentially to provide privacy and a means of defining boundaries—the division between the wilderness and the cultivated—and in the garden itself, a means of dividing flower beds from vegetable patches, terraces from lawn, or, by means of the retaining wall, to make a sloping garden manageable.

Walls have an important functional role to play in our gardens but at the same time offer a unique opportunity for display. In fact, no garden wall should stand naked to the eye, since the beauty of bricks is only enhanced by the luxury of natural vegetation—climbing plants like ivy, wistaria, roses, and clematis are the most obvious contenders for a place on your walls but there are many shrubs, and other plants such as aubrietia, rock-roses, the more tender rhododendrons and azaleas, which grow best when planted by a garden wall; protected from harsh winds they flourish and in turn embellish the protective wall.

Even in small gardens in the heart of the city a wall can look attractive hung with baskets of flowers and trailing plants, and perhaps with an ornamental plaque in metal, terracotta, wood or ceramics.

Laying out

The first step is to decide where you want your wall to be. If it is a free-standing wall, make sure it is square or parallel to the house.

Wall with right-angles

Lay out a cord with short stakes at each end—a building line AB. Use the right-angle square to construct a second building line BC (also a cord with a stake at each end (fig. 1a).

About 4′ (1m) outside the corner stakes erect batter boards. Each will be two 1″ × 6″ (2.5cm × 15cm) boards nailed to three short stakes and set in a right-angle enclosing a corner stake. Lay a long piece of wood with a straight edge across the batter boards. Place the spirit level on this to make sure they are level. Adjust as necessary.

Transfer the cords of the building plan from the corner stakes to nails hammered in the batter boards, using a plumb line to make sure the cords meet precisely over the corner stakes (fig. 1b). Mark the batter boards with nails attached to cords for lines outside the building plan: the edge of the footing and the edge of the footing trench.

Ivy adorning a plain red brick wall—an attractive feature of many old gardens.

The building line will give you an accurate horizontal reference line from which you can measure down to achieve a level trench bottom. Mark the trench and footing lines (see page 30) by dribbling sand over the cords. Remove the cords and the lines will show up clearly the ground. You can now dig out the trench. If you leave the nails in the batter boards, these lines can be reconstructed at any time you wish.

Single wall

If you want to build a free-standing wall without rightangles your layout will be fairly simple but there are other considerations—height, slenderness etc.—which must be taken into account (see page 36).

Place one batter board at either end of your wall length; hammer nails in each of the boards corresponding to your building line, attach a cord to these nails and pull taut. Construct two more lines on the batter boards for the outside edge of the footing and the outside edge of the footing trench. To dig out between the lines, mark with sand, remove the cords but leave nails in place so that the lines can be reconstructed.

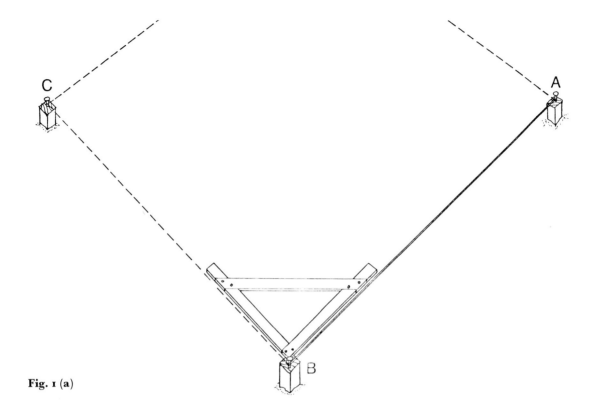

Fig. 1 (a)

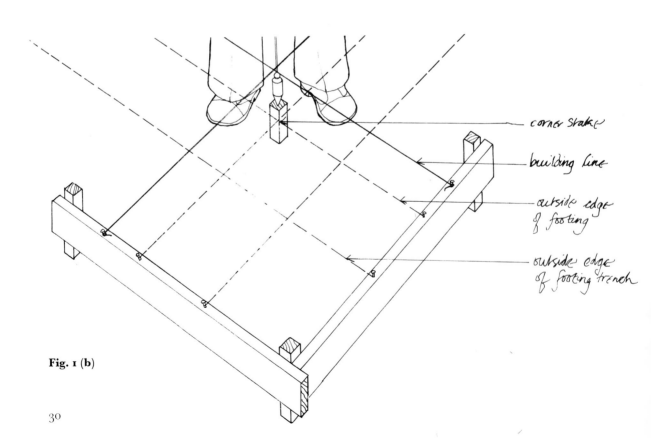

corner stake

building line

outside edge
of footing

outside edge
of footing trench

Fig. 1 (b)

Foundations and footings

The purpose of a foundation is to spread the load from the brickwork evenly over a wide area of ground. The concrete width or footing depends upon the load to be carried and the bearing capacity of the ground. For general purposes, the concrete footing should extend 6″ (15cm) on each side of the wall faces and be 6″ (15cm) thick (figs. 2 and 3). There are two types of foundation: 'strip' and 'trench fill'.

Strip foundation

This is the traditional method (fig. 2). It requires more digging than 'trench fill' but uses far less concrete. When you have laid out the position as described earlier, dig a trench 2′ (60cm) deep and about 2′6″ (76cm) wide. The extra width gives room to work when laying the bricks. Excavate a further trench 6″ (15cm) deep × 1′6″ (46cm) wide in the middle of the first one in which to lay the concrete footing. Ram the trench bottom to compact the soil and drive in wooden stakes, levelling the tops with a straight edge and spirit level (fig. 4). Then pour in concrete up to the level of the tops of the stakes.

For our projects we recommend 'strip' foundation but if you choose 'trench fill' be sure to adjust the number of brick courses below ground accordingly.

The actual foundation depth will depend on your type of soil but should always be below the frostline or below any level where the ground is likely to dry out in summer—generally 2′6″ (76cm) is sufficient. Always check your local building code for depths of foundations.

Trench fill or slab foundation

This method was developed so that mechanical excavators could be used more economically and if the ground is firm enough to support the sides of the excavation it will save you some digging too if you wish to use this method.

You will, on the other hand, need more concrete so we advise ready-mixed. The trench should be 1′6″ (46cm) wide and 1′6″ (46cm) deep. Pour in the concrete almost up to the top of the trench.

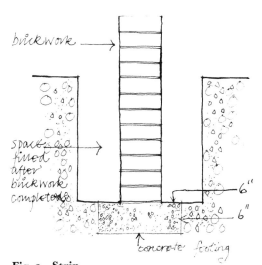

Fig. 2   Strip

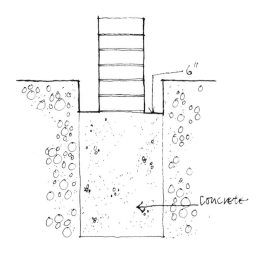

Fig. 3   Trench fill

Achieving a level concrete base for strip foundation

The simplest method of levelling is to use any straight edge and the spirit level. You can use a 1″ × 6″ (2.5cm × 15.2cm) board about 10′ (3m) long if it has a truly straight edge. Drive in a stake close to the angle or at one end of the wall and another almost the length of the straight edge away. Lay the straight edge on the stakes and check with the spirit level. Knock one stake into the ground until a horizontal level is obtained. Then concrete may be poured in up to the top of the stakes.

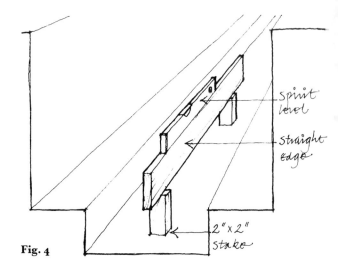

Fig. 4

Stepped foundation for sloping ground

If you are building a site which has a gradient (grade) of 1:12 or more, you may find that, to keep the minimum depth of 2′ (60cm) to the top of concrete, one end will be excessively deep. To avoid this, the concrete can be laid in steps, corresponding approximately to the gradient (grade).

The depth of the steps should be two or more brick courses. Use the horizontal building line, measure along the required distance, say 4′6″ (1.4m) or 6′ (1.8m) and when you are excavating the trench, change the level of the trench bottom at this point, measuring down again from the building line to achieve a level base with steps two or more courses high.

Nail stakes to wooden boards the width of the trench and drive the stakes into the ground. These boards will hold the concrete and form the step in the foundation. They can be removed when the concrete has hardened sufficiently—in this case, about three or four days.

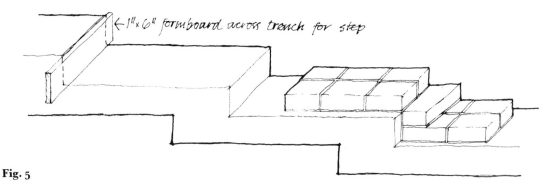

Fig. 5

Brickwork below ground

Bricks suitable for use below ground are some commons, hard or over-burnt bricks, engineering or calcium silicate (sand-lime) bricks or SW bricks.

The mortar to use is one part Portland cement to three parts clean, sharp sand. Sharp sand is quite coarse; the soft fine-grained sand is not suitable for bricklaying. This mix will be difficult to work with and a mortar additive that improves workability can be used; alternatively three or four squirts of liquid detergent will have a similar effect.

Start building from the corner lead (also called the quoin), or ends of the wall using the spirit level to check for vertical and horizontal accuracy, and the square where a right-angle corner is desired. The brickwork should always be bonded for strength. Continue in this way up to two courses below ground level.

The building codes of some states in the U.S. may not permit bricks below ground level. In such cases, the foundation trench will have to be filled with concrete up to ground level and the brickwork started from here on. Always check your local building code to be certain.

Brickwork above ground

Start using the facing bricks two courses below ground still using the same mortar mix (1:3). Build up four courses, bonding the brickwork and checking for verticality and level as you go. The last two courses, which will be above ground, must be jointed, as described on page 38 and a damp-proof course, if required, must be introduced at this level (fig. 6). Having laid the damp-proof course, continue building up the wall from the corner leads or ends, bonding the bricks in alternate courses (see page 37) and checking with the square and spirit level.

The damp-proof course (DPC)

This is an impervious strip and is needed in a wall to prevent damp rising from the ground into the brickwork. In some areas of the U.S. a damp-proof course is not required by the local building code for garden walls. Always check your local code to find out. The damp-proof course, where needed, can be either heavy black PVC (embossed to key to the mortar), or a bituminous non-organic felt which is laid on a mortar bed on top of the bricks. It must be cut to the width of your particular wall. Alternatively, and this is preferred for freestanding walls, two courses of bricks with low-water-absorption laid with the rest of the bricks will give a continuity of strength. Free-standing walls on sheet damp-proof courses are inherently weak and in very high winds can be blown over from that point.

Fig. 6

Sheet DPC **Brick DPC**

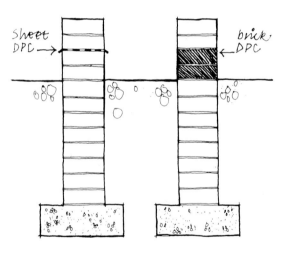

Mixing mortar on a spotboard. Building a simple wall is made easier with two pairs of hands.

How to lay bricks

Bricklaying is not as difficult as it looks, but like any skill, it requires practice, so don't expect miracles the first time you try. Your first attempt at a garden wall may have to be knocked down, but if you do this before the mortar is dry, you can clean off the bricks and only a few shovels of mortar will have been wasted.

Remember, how you lay your bricks will depend on your choice of bond pattern (see page 37) which will be decided partly by the strength required for your particular wall.

You have now dug your foundations, placed your concrete, let it dry, and are ready to lay your first course of bricks. Be sure to have read about tools, cutting a brick, mixing mortar and damp-proof courses on pages 26 and 33. Stretch a building line to mark where the face of the wall is to be. If it is dry weather, moisten your bricks—they should feel slightly damp, but not wet, and off you go.

Note: brickwork should be covered at night if there is any danger of frost. Any brickwork less than two days old which has been frosted must be taken down and rebuilt as the frost will have permanently weakened the mortar which will then have no cohesion.

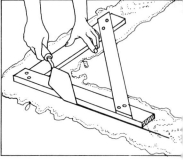

1   Drop mortar onto foundation and spread it roughly along line of wall ½″ (1.3cm) thick. Plumbing down from line and using square as guide, mark line of wall on mortar bed with trowel

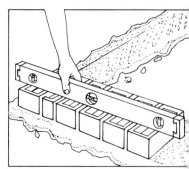

5   Check that the line is level.

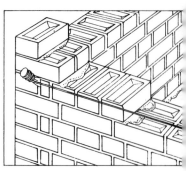

9   Using line as guide, build up rest of wall. Fix the pins or nails into mortar joint at ends and, keeping line ⅜″ (1cm) clear of wall, move it up as you go.

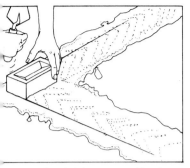

Place first brick at corner 'frog' uppermost (if there is one) and tap to place.

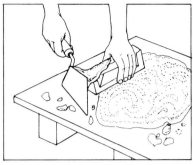

3 'Butter' end or side of next brick about $\frac{1}{2}''$ (1.3cm) thick, set it next to first brick and tap into place.

closet brick

4 Each joint should be filled with mortar, with a little squeezing out, to give $\frac{3}{8}''$ (1cm) mortar joint.

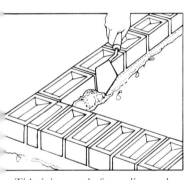

Tidy joints ready for tooling and as you go along and try to ensure all vertical joints are equal, about $\frac{3}{8}''$ (1cm). Keep face of bricks as free of mortar as possible.

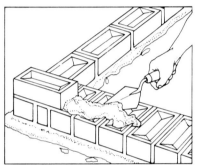

7 Lay second course of bricks on first, (mortar between the two should be $\frac{3}{8}''$ [1cm]) observing the arrangement required by your chosen bond.

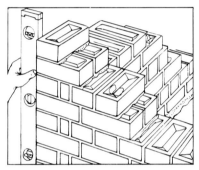

8 Build up corners or ends of wall first, using gauge rod to ensure brick courses rise correctly and spirit level to check verticality.

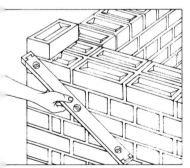

Keep checking that wall isn't bulging by using spirit level held at an angle.

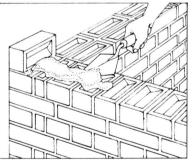

11 For a simple coping spread mortar again for bricks laid on edge.

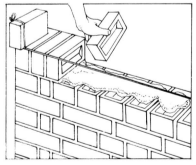

12 Place end bricks in position. Wind line round spare brick and stretch to other end as guide for remainder of course.

Free-standing walls

Any free-standing wall, that is a wall unattached to any other structure has a tendency to tip over. The thickness of a wall in relation to its height (slenderness ratio) and its length are all limiting factors in the construction of walls. For stability, a free-standing wall should not exceed certain heights without piers (pilasters) built up with it (see photo and fig. 7). The table below shows the required position and size of pier for two wall thicknesses—half-brick and one brick thick, according to height. The piers (pilasters) form part of the wall from the foundation upwards and the concrete foundation must be set to allow for the additional width at the positions in which they occur.

Sometimes a half-brick wall can only have a good face on one side owing to irregularities in the actual brick manufacture, so decide which face is the most attractive. The piers (pilasters) can usually be avoided on the good side, but in the case of a party or boundary walls, legal considerations may be a limiting factor.

height	thickness	position of piers	projection of piers
up to 3′ (90cm)	half brick	6′ centres	half brick
(90cm)	one brick	not needed	
3′ to 4′6″ (90cm to 1.3m)	half brick	6′ centres	one brick
	one brick	not needed	
4′6″ to 6′ (1.3m to 1.8m)	half brick	6′ centres	one brick
	one brick	9′ centres	one brick

Half-brick piers (pilasters) projecting at intervals along the length of a wall.

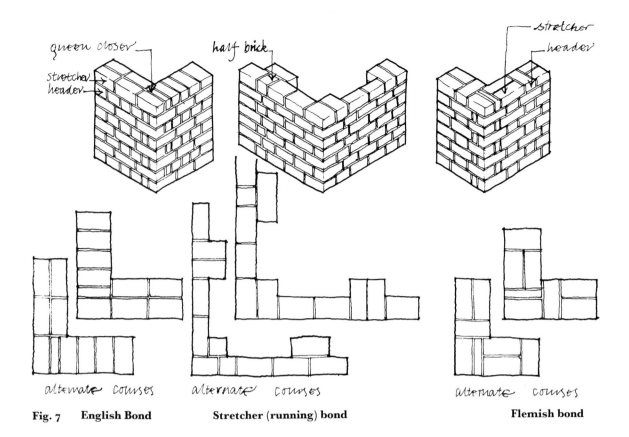

Fig. 7   **English Bond**   **Stretcher (running) bond**   **Flemish bond**

Bonding

Bonding is the word used to describe the interlocking of the bricks; it gives strength to a large panel basically composed of small pieces.

In the introductory pages different types of bond, e.g. English, Flemish, were illustrated. In addition to its primary function of locking the bricks together, bonding has a part to play in how the wall looks.

Successful bonding means not placing the joints between the bricks directly above one another since this would weaken the wall. To avoid this and at all times maintain equal spacing, it is often necessary to cut bricks in half lengthways; these half bricks are referred to as queen closers (fig. 7). They are used in each alternate course at the ends or corner leads to maintain the overlap necessary to ensure that each brick rests equally on at least two bricks.

English bond. A one-brick-thick wall built in English bond is the easiest arrangement to remember: it has alternate header and stretcher courses. Spacing at the corners or 'stopped' end is adjusted by using queen closers in each header course.

Flemish bond. A one-brick-thick wall built in Flemish bond has alternate headers and stretchers in each course. Corners or 'stopped' ends are spaced with quarter bats (bricks cut in quarters widthways) or queen closers adjacent to the first header in each alternate course.

Stretcher (running) bond. A half-brick-thick wall in stretcher (running) bond has the bricks in each alternate course staggered so that the vertical joints occur over the centre of a brick. Half bats (bricks cut in half widthways) are used to bond the piers (pilasters). Stretcher (running) bond is popular today because it avoids the difficulty of bonding. As a half-brick stretcher wall is not very strong, it is usual to build a one-brick wall in two stretcher bond 'skins' (wythes) with the two skins (wythes) reinforced with metal ties (see page 40).

Other effects can be obtained by variations of bond. Textured patterns can be achieved by setting a regular pattern of bricks so that they project about $\frac{1}{2}''$ (1.2cm) from the general face. Fig.

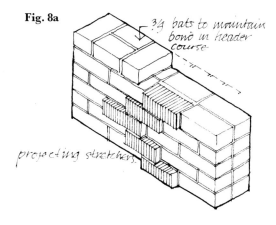

Fig. 8a

34 bats to maintain bond in header course

projecting stretchers

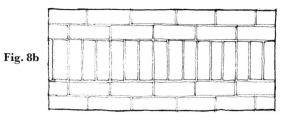

Fig. 8b

8a shows a pattern of stretchers projecting in English garden wall bond. English garden wall bond is similar to English bond but has header courses every sixth course; those between are stretcher courses. It is not as strong as English or Flemish bond.

Fig. 8b shows a course of bricks on end laid in a stretcher bond wall. The vertical bricks (bricks on end) are backed with three courses of stretchers.

Pointing, jointing and tooling

This is the finishing treatment of the exposed mortar joints. It is done firstly to ensure that all horizontal and vertical joints are solidly filled with mortar to keep them watertight: secondly, for decorative reasons—the appearance can be varied by recessed or coloured mortar pointing.

Usually, except if coloured mortar is to be used, brickwork is tooled as it is laid and this is correctly called 'jointing'. The joints are filled with mortar and then finished in one of a number of ways. The mortar can be struck off with the edge of the bricklayer's trowel blade, called 'flush' jointing (fig. 9a); the joints may be 'weathered' (fig. 9b) or tooled with a bent $\frac{3}{8}''$ (1cm) diameter steel rod (bucket-handle; fig. 9c) or recessed from the surface (fig. 9d). Recessed joints look attractive but should only be used with well-burnt bricks which are less likely to be damaged as a result of water freezing on the top edges of the bricks. A square-ended piece of hardwood is all that is required. Rake out the joint about $\frac{1}{2}''$ (1.2cm) deep when the mortar has begun to harden, say half an hour after laying, and shape with the piece of wood. When you are jointing, try to avoid smearing the face of the brick with mortar as this will look unsightly and is difficult to clean off when dry. In all cases the mortar will dry to a lighter colour. You can add different colours to your brickwork with coloured mortars; this is called 'pointing' and in this case the joints should be raked out as the wall is built and pointed afterwards.

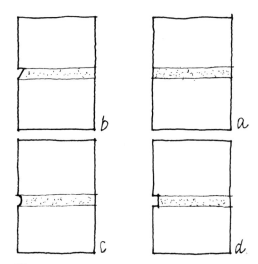

Fig. 9

Copings

A top is needed for a wall to throw off rainwater and protect the brickwork below from being saturated and exposed to frost action: this is called the 'coping'.

Traditional copings had a slight overhang each side of the wall face with a groove called a throating on the underside (figs. 10a and b). Rainwater would drip off the edge without running down the face of the brickwork. The principle also applies to tile copings often done with pantiles (fig. 10c). Two rows of flat tiles bedded in mortar under a brick-on-edge (rowlock) coping is also common—this is known as a 'creasing' (fig. 10d).

These methods are not popular today; a flush coping (fig. 10e) is preferred for aesthetic reasons. It does not, however, offer the same protection and staining may occur at the top of the wall. In all cases a damp-proof course must be provided before the coping is put on, to prevent water saturating the wall and the subsequent possibility of frost damage. Use either heavy black PVC or bituminous non-organic felt and lay this one course below a brick-on-edge coping to give a better bedding to the bricks. Use a 1:3 mortar mix for copings and lay the bricks as shown on pages 34-5. Before placing the first and last brick at each end, build a metal cramp into the mortar to curve around these bricks and help keep them in place.

Brick planter and wall on radial paving. The wall shows a simple brick-on-edge coping with three half-bricks at each end held on by metal cramps. Notice the mitred bricks which form very neat corners. The planter in the background also has a brick-on-edge coping, and the mortar joints on the outside face are thicker than normal to allow for the curvature.

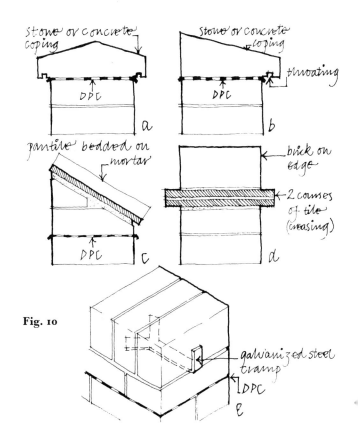

Fig. 10

Recessed pointing.

Cavity walls

Walls that enclose a room, as in a house extension let's say, must be able to stop rain penetrating through to the inside face and keep heat in as well. A *solid* brick wall is not capable of doing either of these things and so the 'cavity' wall was devised. This is a wall built in two 'skins' (wythes) with a 2″ (5cm) cavity in between.

The outer skin is built in facing brickwork half-brick thick and laid stretcher bond. The inner skin should be built in lightweight insulating concrete blocks. These measure 1′6″ × 1′ (45cm × 30cm) and are available in thicknesses of 3″ (7.5cm), 4″ (10cm), 6″ (15cm) and 8″ (20cm). It is usual to use 4″ (10cm) blocks for cavity walls. The two skins are tied together with glavanized cavity wall ties. Wall ties are set in the wall at 3′ (90cm) centres horizontally every sixth course in alternate rows. They should be staggered. There must be nothing, except for the ties themselves, to bridge the air space as this will enable water to travel across to the inner skin. It is therefore of the utmost importance that no mortar droppings should be allowed to fall into the cavity as they may rest on the ties and form a bridge across which water may pass.

The bottom part of the cavity below ground is filled with mortar with the top sloped to the outer skin to allow water to run off.

A separate damp-proof course must be provided for each skin.

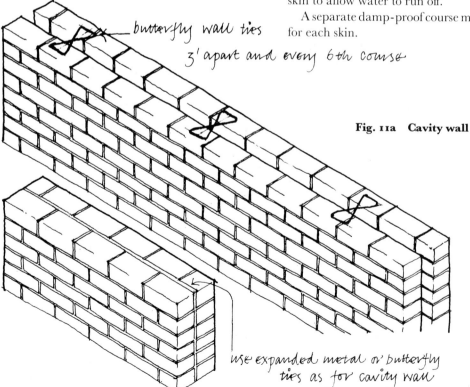

butterfly wall ties

3′ apart and every 6th course

Fig. 11a   Cavity wall

use expanded metal or butterfly ties as for cavity wall

Fig. 11b   Wall built as two stretcher (running) bond wythes

Alcove walls

Our sketch shows a type of wall whose shape alone is sufficient to provide the stiffening necessary to prevent overturning—we call this an 'alcove wall'. The alcoves can be used as niches for statues or plants, or for seats if stone slabs or wooden slats are built in as in our garden seat on page 96.

For an alcove wall 6′ (1.8m) high, the panel of plain wall between recesses should not be more than 6′ (1.8m) in length.

Excavate the foundation as described earlier but, if your soil is very soft, if may not be possible to excavate the trench without something supporting the sides of the excavation. If so, make rough wooden boxes 2′ (high) × 1′6″ × 6″ (60cm × 45cm) and place them in the trench (fig. 12). By doing this you will avoid using an unnecessary amount of concrete in the foundation and the wooden boxes can be used over again.

Lay the concrete 6″ (15cm) thick in the trench up to the top of the box and lay the bricks exactly as described earlier (pages 34-5). Remember, however, that the right-angle square should be no more than about 2′ (60cm) long to fit in the recesses when you are checking the squareness of the internal angles.

When laying the first course of bricks, check with the straight edge that the front and back

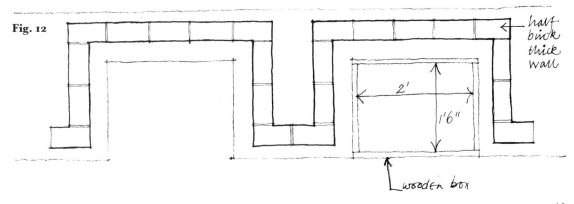

Fig. 12

half brick thick wall

2′

1′6″

wooden box

panels are in alignment. Continue to check this as the wall is being built, not forgetting of course to use the spirit level for vertical and horizontal accuracy.

Build in a damp-proof course unless this is not required by your local building code.

The coping should be one course of engineering or SW bricks bedded flat. A $1\frac{1}{4}''$ (3.5cm) paving brick could be used to give a thin line finish to the top of the wall.

Remember that half-brick brickwork can only have a good face one side.

If recessed pointing is used this must only be on the fair face and should not be recessed more than $\frac{1}{4}''$ (6mm), or the stability of the wall may be reduced.

The famous serpentine wall at the University of Virginia in Charlottesville, designed by Thomas Jefferson.

Serpentine walls

The serpentine shape is another way of 'building in' stiffening to a wall without buttresses or piers (pilasters). It gives a soft flowing line to a long unbroken surface, but it should only be used on a fairly flat site. This kind of wall has often been used for the boundary walls of country estates.

The curved foundation is more difficult to lay out than straight lines and right-angles, and much will depend on reasonably accurate judgment by eye.

Begin by laying two parallel cords 3′6″ (1m) apart in the position of the wall and drive stout stakes into the ground at 16′ (5m) centres along one cord and at the same intervals along the other cord but occuring midway between the opposite stakes. Using these stakes as a guide, excavate the trench 2′ (60cm) wide, following a wavy line.

The wall should be built one brick thick and English garden wall bond would be suitable (see page 37).

To help you get the curves in the brickwork, make templates from a piece of $\frac{3}{4}$″ (2cm) plywood 8′ (2.5m) long × 3′ (90cm) wide cut as shown in fig. 13. They can be used to lay out the first course of bricks and as a guide as the rest of the wall is built.

Finish the wall with a brick-on-edge coping and joint in any of the ways described on page 38.

A simple curved wall with radial paving.

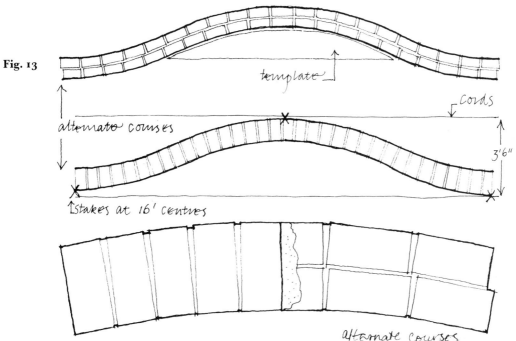

Fig. 13

template

cords

alternate courses

3′6″

stakes at 16′ centres

alternate courses

43

Open screen walls

A variety of exciting designs can be created by an imaginative arrangement of bricks and space. We have illustrated a variety of patterns which are fairly easy to achieve. The open screen is useful in providing some shelter from wind or for privacy, while allowing a view through.

Open screen walls should be buttressed the same way as solid walls but, as they do not offer the same resistance to wind pressure, they are less likely to be blown over. If a very open design is chosen, however, it would be better to use it in combination with solid panels and piers (pilasters).

(For screen wall and carport project see page 108.)

Below: Seventeenth-century ornate open brickwork walling. Strictly for the professionals.

Opposite left: A simple screen wall.

Opposite right: Large bricks laid flat to form elaborate screen walling.

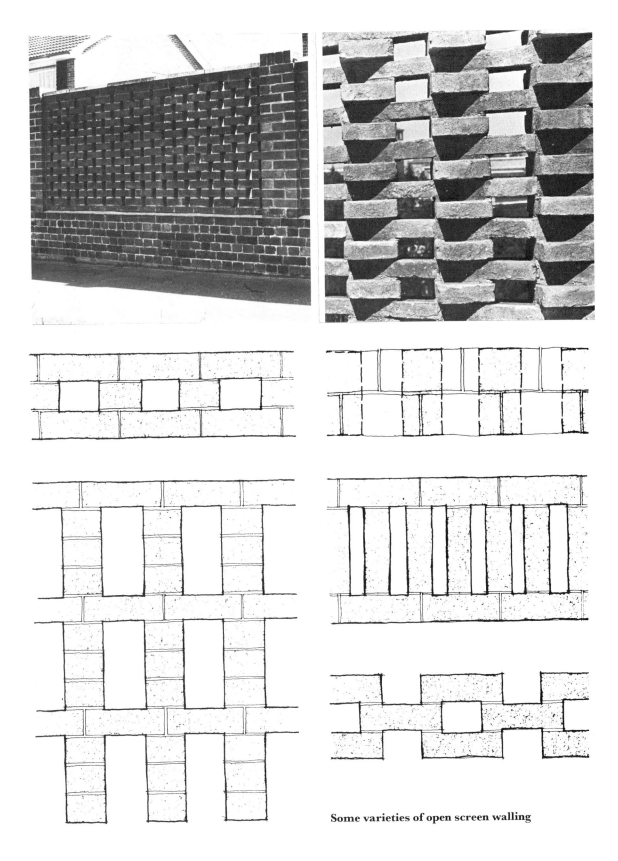

Some varieties of open screen walling

45

Retaining walls

Brickwork is a traditional means of making retaining walls and steps. The colours of the bricks, if carefully chosen, can blend in naturally and harmoniously with the surrounding garden areas. The small unit size of a brick means that all kinds of steps can be accommodated—shallow flights with 3″ (7.5cm) risers can make pushing or pulling a barrow full of compost or plants up and down the garden relatively easy.

Different levels can add great interest even to a small garden. In fact, the smaller the space, the more important it is to create height and width with retaining walls and one or two steps. For anyone nearing retirement and looking for easily maintained garden features, raised beds with retaining walls are a great convenience. The high level keeps the soil and the plants from encroaching on the path, and makes sweeping and tidying much easier. If the walls are built up to 2′ (60cm) or 2½′ (76cm), the strain of bending over to work is practically abolished. And then there is the pleasure of growing wall plants and even rock plants in

special pockets left in the wall—hanging baskets can be something of a nuisance to care for and water, but walls with hanging flowers planted along the top give all the colour and foliage patterns with none of the disadvantages. Through a number of changes in level you can create small terraces and so utilize height as well as the flat two-dimensional area on the ground.

As its name implies, a retaining wall serves to hold back earth. The same principles of dynamics govern a huge reinforced concrete dam and a 2′ (60cm) high retaining garden wall, as their functions are similar: to stop water or earth at a high level from spilling over uncontrollably to a lower level. Examples of retaining walls can be seen in subways and railway cuttings; the walls of any basement are also retaining walls.

Fig. 14 shows how the ground at a higher level exerts pressure or thrust against the wall, tending to push it over. This pressure increases as the difference in height between levels increases as well as with the amount of water in the ground;

obviously, water tending to flow to a lower level will push against the wall unless an escape route is provided. As the problems increase with height we will keep our retaining wall to 3′ (90cm) maximum—a small wall which can be used for terracing.

A retaining wall will remain generally damp because of the water always in the ground. This can be used to advantage. Lichens will grow on the face of the wall and if you leave open joints or pockets in the brickwork, a wide variety of alpine plants can be grown there.

There will be no point in laying a damp-proof course in a retaining wall such as this because of its continual dampness (fig. 15). You can, however, if you wish, give the inside face of the wall two coats of a bituminous compound.

Use a 1:2:4 concrete mix for the foundations. The concrete footing should be not less than 6″ (15cm) thick and 1′9″ (53cm) wide for a one-brick-thick wall.

The choice of brick is important; it should not be a very soft brick. The best choice is a brick with low water-absorption properties, a hard-burnt rough stock or SW brick. Use a 1:½:3 mortar mix.

The wall itself is built in a similar manner to that described on pages 34 and 35, using a bond such as English or Flemish which gives suitable strength (fig. 15).

Foundations

Dig a foundation trench as described on page 31, laying out the position with cords and batter boards. Dig to a depth 2′6″ (76cm) below the finished ground level of the lower part. The actual depth will of course depend on the slope of the ground. In the case of terracing see fig. 17.

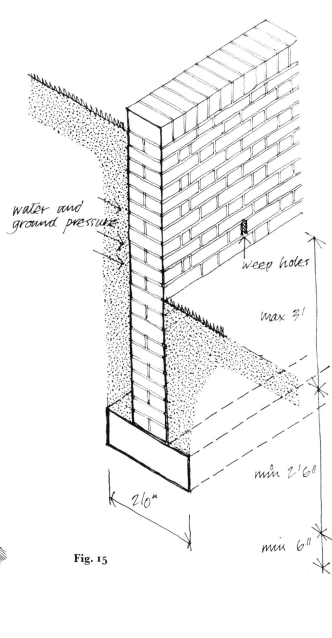

water and ground pressure

weep holes

max 3′

min 2′6″

2′0″

min 6″

Fig. 15

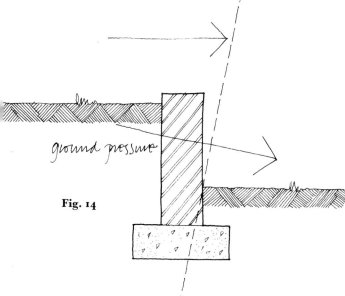

ground pressure

Fig. 14

47

DRAINAGE

Groundwater will exert a pressure tending to overturn the wall and must be allowed to drain through to the lower level. This can be achieved in two ways: either leave open joints in the brick or build in short lengths of clay pipes. These openings are called 'weep-holes'.

Pipes are more effective than open joints which may eventually become blocked, particularly if the ground contains gravelly clay. For a retaining wall 3′ (90cm) high the opening should be two or three courses above the lower ground level. Either leave the vertical joint between bricks open and free of mortar, at intervals of 3′ (90cm) (fig 16a) or build lengths of 3″ (7.5cm) diameter clay pipe into the wall every 6′ (1.8m) bedded in mortar and tipping about $\frac{1}{2}″$ (1.2cm) downwards (fig. 16b).

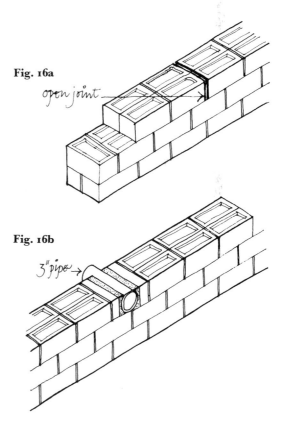

Fig. 16a

open joint

Fig. 16b

3″ pipe →

Retaining wall and steps.

Terracing

If you have a sloping site which is unacceptable for visual or practical reasons, you may wish to 'terrace' it, i.e. level it in sections, each slightly lower than the one above, with the ground in between horizontal. 'Terracing' is often used by hillside communities as a means of making the ground easier to cultivate: without it, the top soil would be washed down the hillside by heavy rains.

While these conditions are not likely to occur in your garden, there are other reasons why 'terracing' would be an asset; grass-cutting, for example, is made much easier when there are only flat areas to mow. Visual interest can be increased and a more imaginative planting scheme developed for the garden because you will be working with a three-dimensional ground area instead of a tilted flat plane.

The usual terracing method is 'cut and fill'. As seen in fig. 17, the higher part of the ground is 'cut' away and the soil used to raise the level of the lower part.

The change of level should not be more than 3' (90cm) for reasons of stability. The height, together with the degree of slope will determine the distance between retaining walls.

Laying out

To obtain the distance between levels, drive a long stake into the ground leaving 3' (90cm) (or less if you want a lower wall) above ground. Place a long straight edge on the stake, use the spirit-level to check when it is horizontal and mark the point where the other end touches the ground.

Mark out the position of the first retaining wall with cord and batter boards and dig a trench a minimum of 3'6" (1m) deep × 2' (60cm) wide at the bottom. Pour the concrete for the foundation and when this has set build the wall up to existing ground level and then to not more than 3' (90cm). Strip the top soil and put in a heap to be used later. Then excavate the soil at the higher level and place lower down the site, tamping 6" (15cm) layers to consolidate the earth and avoid depressions appearing later. Spread the top soil, rake and roll and, if a lawn is what you want, it is now ready for seeding.

Terracing in the Judean Hills near Jerusalem. These low stone walls create numerous flat levels so allowing the steep hillside to be successfully cultivated.

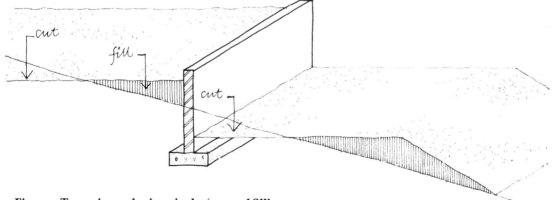

Fig. 17   Terracing a sloping site by 'cut and fill'

Steps

With a change in ground level is will almost certainly be necessary to provide steps. Where steps form part of a building such as an entrance to a house or room extension they will be controlled by construction practice concerning the height of the riser (R) which is the vertical distance or height of the step and the tread (T) which is the horizontal distance between two risers. (Actual tread width may exceed this distance if there is a small overhang of the tread over the riser. This overhang is called the 'nosing'). Figs. 19a and b show alternative methods of making brick steps— with and without a nosing. If the following formula is used, the steps should satisfy any code requirements: $2R + T = 22''$ to $28''$ (56cm to 71cm). However, if the steps do not form part of a building— and they would not in the case of a garden retaining wall and steps—regulations don't apply and there is greater flexibility.

Outdoors there is generally much more space available and a much broader tread width can be accommodated.

To avoid discomfort, the riser should not be less

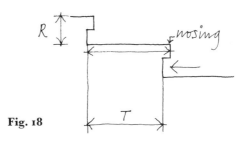

Fig. 18

than $6''$ (15cm) and not more than $8''$ (20cm), and it is very important to make sure that all risers are the same height.

The greater the overall width of the steps can be (that is from side to side) relative to the overall height, the more visually attractive the wall and steps will look. Where possible, aim for a width of between $9'$ (2.7m) and $12'6''$ (3.6m) for a wall height of $3'$ (90cm) and not narrower than $4'6''$ (1.35m).

Fig. 20 shows two alternative ways in which the steps can be formed, with $6''$ (15cm) risers. The

Brick steps can be made in a variety of ways. Here the risers are formed with two courses of bricks laid with the narrow face outwards, the brick-on-edge treads are laid on top.

height of the riser can be adjusted by either varying the thickness of the packing (fig. 19a) or increasing the size of the vertical cut brick (fig. 19b). The steps in figs. 20a and b are formed as shown in fig. 19b, with a small overhang (nosing) of the brick treads, giving a shadow line which helps, particularly at dusk, to define the edge of the step.

As seen in fig. 20b, for a change in level of 3′ (90cm) using a 6″ (15cm) riser and step with a nosing, the return end walls will be 7′9″ (2.36m) from the face of the retaining wall. These should be constructed along with the wall itself and you should leave the space between these end walls unexcavated except for stripping the top soil, as the slope already existing will be used for the steps.

Casting the concrete steps

You must first cast the rough concrete steps on which the bricks will be laid. The wet concrete will have to be supported by lengths of board or 'forms' as it sets. Use 1¼″ × 6″ (3.2cm × 15cm) wooden boards nailed to 2″ × 2″ (5cm × 5cm) stakes driven very firmly into the ground. The stakes should not be more than 3′ (90cm) apart. Before doing this, cover the inside face of the return end walls with polythene to prevent concrete splashes on the brickwork.

Check the boards with the spirit level to make sure they are level and that the top edge of the lower board is in line with the bottom edge of the next board up (fig. 20a).

Now lay hardcore (or gravel) on the slope about 4″ (10cm) thick and ram this quite thoroughly taking care not to disturb the forms.

Pour the concrete and finish by tamping the top surface of each step with the edge of a board.

Leave the concrete to harden for at least three days before removing the forms and laying the bricks.

The bricks for the steps may be the same type as those used for the walling or they may be different for visual contrast; they must, however, have similar properties. Further information on suitable bricks can be found in the section on brick paving.

Laying the bricks

Start with the bottom riser. The bricks for the risers will probably have to be cut to fit. Bed them against the concrete in mortar with the narrow face to the front of the step. Next lay the bottom tread, one course of bricks on edge, again bedding each brick in mortar as you go. Continue with the remaining treads and risers as shown in fig. 20b, making sure that all the joints in both treads and risers are in line with one another. Strike a flush joint as you go. The top tread should be level with the brick-on-edge (rowlock header course) coping at the top of the wall (fig. 20b).

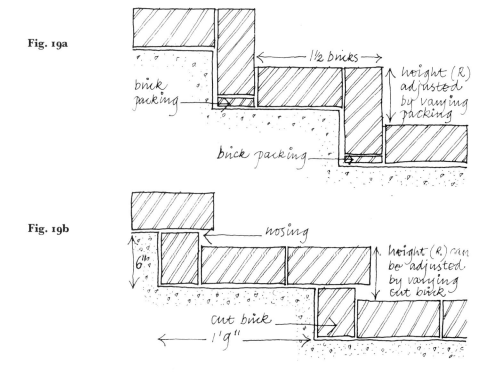

Fig. 19a

Fig. 19b

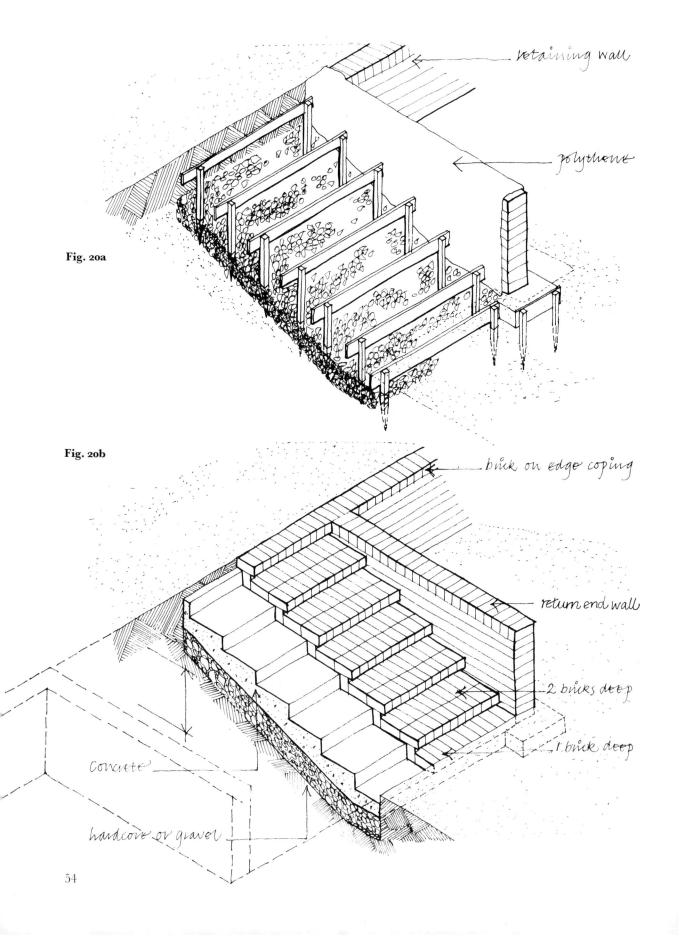

Fig. 20a

retaining wall

polythene

Fig. 20b

brick on edge coping

return end wall

2 bricks deep

1 brick deep

Concrete

hardcore or gravel

Mitred corners

Where steps or coping form a corner, it is sometimes desirable, for a neat appearance, to use mitred bricks. 'Mitring' is the term used to describe cutting bricks to an angle. 45° is the most usual angle required (see photograph) but sometimes, as in our Summer House project, bricks will have to be cut to a wider or narrower angle.

The way to cut the bricks is either by adapting the bat and closer gauge (see page 25), or by marking the bricks to the correct angle with a wax crayon and cutting with a brick saw. The bat-and-closer gauge method will save you a lot of time if the amount of cutting is large. Always mitre-cut first and then cut the bricks to the required length.

45° mitred angle to brick steps.

Pavings
and patios

Well-planned walks and paths are essential elements of garden design; they are the main arteries of our gardens and present a lasting impression to visitors and guests.

Strong, even surfaces with good drainage, tidy edges and a feeling of space are the basic requirements for satisfactory wear, comfort and visual appeal. Paths should be wide—not just slim trickles through the undergrowth, but wide enough for two people to walk comfortably abreast. Brick-paved paths are usually popular with experienced gardeners for their ease of maintenance and weeding, so long as the bricks are set low enough not to interfere with the mowing of grass verges.

Paving near the house is of great value practically and visually. You can create an outdoor living room, a private terrace off a bedroom or an area for cooking, eating or just lying in the sun. Small city gardens can look tidy and attractive if completely paved, perhaps with steps to create different levels. A large patio or terrace will take quite a lot of bricks. If you wish to pave an area 16′ × 40′ (4.8m × 12.1m) you will need almost 2000 bricks if laid flat, and 3000 if laid on edge. But once they are down, the advantages are enormous.

The patio needs no upkeep, looks good, and provides a link between the house and garden in a pleasing and logical way. If the paving is bedded on sand, with sand in the joints, the paving pattern can be changed whenever you wish—you only need to destroy one brick and the rest will come out as good as new.

In some countries of northern Europe, notably Holland and Belgium, bricks for paving have long been recognized as a durable and easy paving material, even for roads taking heavy urban traffic. The U.S. also has not been slow to recognize the

Any opening in paving looks neater finished off with edging. Here a running bond pattern is neatened with radiating bricks on edge.

benefits of brick roads—Lombard Street in San Francisco is probably the most famous brick-paved road in the world, and certainly the crookedest.

Whatever the situation, there is a colour and strength of brick and a paving pattern to suit it but whether the area to be paved is small or large, or the paving intended for domestic or industrial use, bricks must be chosen and laid with an eye to design, durability and over-all effect.

Joint pattern plays an important part in the appearance of any kind of brickwork. Because some of the practical aspects which limit the possibilities in wall construction do not apply in paving, there is more opportunity to be imaginative.

Some bond patterns are 'directional', i.e. the eye is directed along the line of the unbroken joints. Examples of directional patterns are running bond, and herringbone laid diagonally. Others are 'static', i.e. the pattern does not give the impression of movement. Examples are basketweave and stack bond (jack-on-jack). Try to use the movement in a pattern to direct the eye to a focal point like a statue, or through patio doors.

Before you make a decision about which paving pattern to choose, ask yourself the following questions:

1 Does the face size of your chosen brick give the scale of pattern desired or should a second scale be superimposed with a different bond or different paving material? (See page 76.)

2 Will the pattern involve special units or an unacceptable amount of cutting? (Bear in mind that edge-cutting becomes relatively less important as areas increase in size.)

3 Is a directional pattern required, e.g. to emphasize a particular route—through a garden, through patio doors, or to provide water run-off areas where there is not much of a slope?

4 Is a good interlocking pattern required to prevent the paving from shifting as a result of use by cars?

How to lay a paving

Getting started

Thickness has little practical effect on the performance and durability of paving: the choice of brick, a good base, and even bedding are the important requirements for long and satisfactory wear. When you are considering suitable paving bricks, you have two basic possibilities. Firstly, there are purpose-made paving bricks and secondly, suitable standard bricks. The first category includes many different shapes, sizes and colours and you should visit a showroom if at all possible in order to get an idea of the vast range. If you chose standard bricks, they must have a high frost resistance. All hard-pressed clay bricks that have low water-absorption properties can be used, and many other bricks which fall into the category of 'facing and common bricks of special quality' including solid wire-cut or stock bricks. You can lay your bricks either on edge or flat but if you use bricks with perforations or frogs, make sure they are used on edge. Unsuitable bricks are soft or under-burnt bricks.

Owing to the large variety of colour, shape and texture available for paving bricks today, you would be well advised to consult the experts over the type of brick you need for your particular area, taking into account the kind of bedding you intend to use and the particular drainage problems. In the U.K. the people to consult are the Brick Development Association and in the U.S., the Brick Institute of America. They exist to advise architects and engineers but will be happy to help you too and give you details and recommend which manufacturer to consult.

The base

The long-term success of any paving, whether a simple patio for tables and chairs or a pathway leading to a carport, depends on a good base. leading to a carport, depends on a good base. There are two basic methods: 'bedding on sand for patios and pathways used only for walking and 'bedding on concrete and hardcore (or gravel)' which should be used if the paving is intended for cars, since in this case a more solid foundation is necessary.

The extent of drainage needed will depend on which method of base is chosen. If you are using method 1 'bedding on sand and hardcore (or gravel)', there will be sufficient drainage through the sand layer and hardcore (or gravel), if the subsoil drainage is adequate. If you are using method 2 'concrete and hardcore (or gravel)', you will have to create a gradient (grade) for water run-off if the site is not sufficiently sloping.

Tools	Materials	
Canvas work gloves	Bricks 32 per sq yd (36 per m²)—laid flat	
Bricklayer's trowel	48 per sq yd (54 per m²)—on edge	
Spirit level		
Broad-faced hammer	*Method 1*	*Method 2*
Brick set	**per sq yd (m²) of paving**	**per sq yd (m²) of paving**
Long piece of wood with a straight edge	Hardcore (or gravel) $\frac{1}{8}$ cu yd (m³)	Hardcore (or gravel) $\frac{1}{8}$ cu yd (m³)
Soil rammer	Sand $\frac{1}{19}$ cu yd (m³)	Cement (see estimating table)
Tamping board		Sand $\frac{1}{10}$ cu yd (m³)
		$1'' \times 6''$ (2.5cm × 15cm) and $2'' \times 2''$ (5cm × 5cm) wood for forms.

Bands of brick successfully break up a flat concrete walkway in this urban shopping area.

Bedding on sand and hardcore (or gravel)

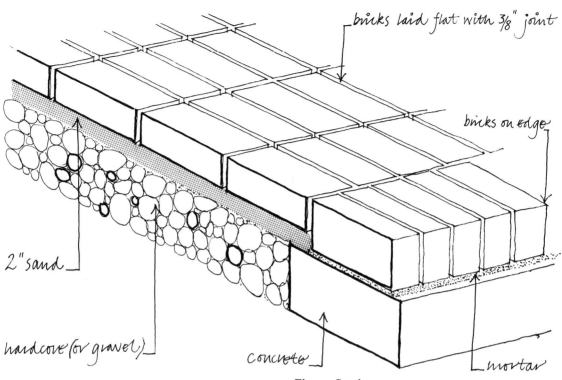

bricks laid flat with 3/8" joint

bricks on edge

2" sand

hardcore (or gravel)

concrete

mortar

Fig. 1 Section

If the paving is to abut the house, the finished level of paving should be 6″ (15cm) below any damp-proof course in the house wall. Look for this between brick courses approximately at floor level: it generally shows up as a somewhat thicker mortar joint. Excavate the earth to a depth of 9″ (23cm) below the intended level of paving and, to prevent the future growth of long-rooted weeds such as dandelions, apply a strong weedkiller, but be careful to keep this out of the reach of children and pets.

When laying bricks on this type of base, you will need to provide some support at the edges. This can be provided by nailing two 1″ × 6″ (2.5cm × 15cm) boards 1′6″ (46cm) apart to 2″ × 2″ (5cm × 5cm) stakes and casting a concrete edging. Check the level of the board top edges with the spirit level and tamp the concrete across (fig. 2).

Spread hardcore (or gravel) to a depth of 4″ (10cm) over the whole area within the concrete edges and ram to compact it. Hardcore is broken

Fig. 2 1″ × 6″ boards supported by stakes for casing concrete edging

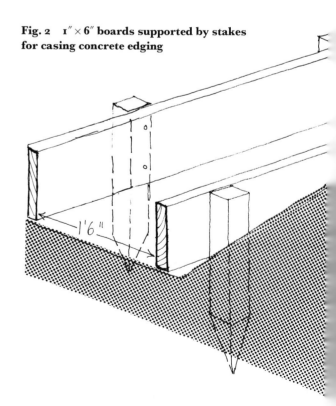

1′6″

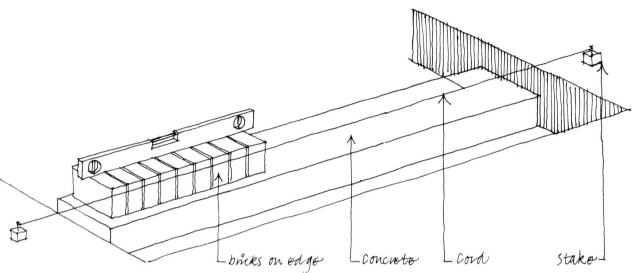

Fig. 3   Laying the edging

brick or stone rubble, the largest pieces of which are around 3″ (7.5cm). If this is not available, use gravel. The more it is compacted, the better the base and the less likelihood there will be of depressions appearing in the finished paving.

Now set out a base line with stakes and cord corresponding to the required finished level and length of your paving (fig. 3). Lay your edging course of bricks (they can be laid flat or on edge) bedding and jointing them in mortar using a 1:½:3 mix. Check frequently with the spirit level to ensure a level top.

Now haunch the brick edging with concrete 1:2:4 as in fig 4. Spread and level building sand over the hardcore (or gravel) to a thickness of 2½″ (6cm) and rake over to allow the sand to settle and fill any remaining voids in the hardcore (or gravel). One cubic yard (metre³) of sand will cover 12 square yards (metre²). This type of base will be self-draining if you use sand for the joints (see jointing, page 65). You are now ready to lay your bricks which can be laid flat or on edge.

Fig. 4   Detail of haunched edging

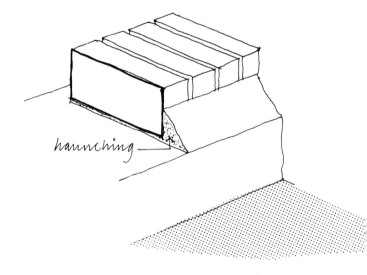

Bedding on concrete and hardcore (or gravel)

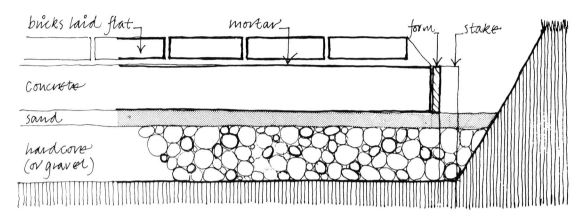

Fig. 5　Section

This method of bedding should be used if the paving is intended for cars or any situation where a tougher base is required. It is not self-draining and adequate drainage must be provided by means of a gradient (grade) (see page 64).

Excavate the earth to a depth of 1′2″ (36cm) below the required level for the finished paving. Consolidate the earth with the rammer, then construct the forms which will define the peri-

meters of the paving and hold the concrete while it sets.

You will need pieces of 1″ × 6″ (2.5cm × 15cm) and 2″ × 2″ (5cm × 5cm) wood, cut in lengths of about 2′ (60cm) with one end roughly pointed. It is best to use second-hand wood since after using it for casting concrete you will not be able to use it for any other jobs.

Before placing the forms, lay out the perimeter

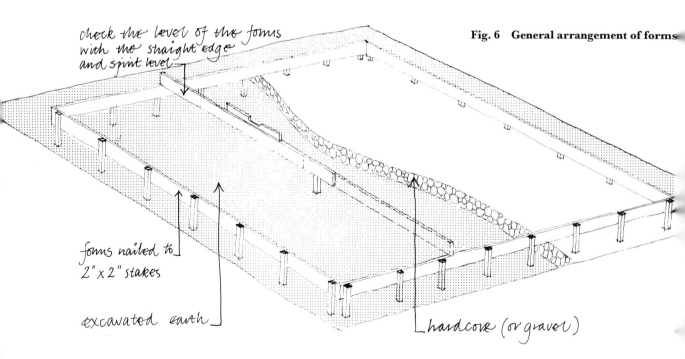

Fig. 6　General arrangement of forms

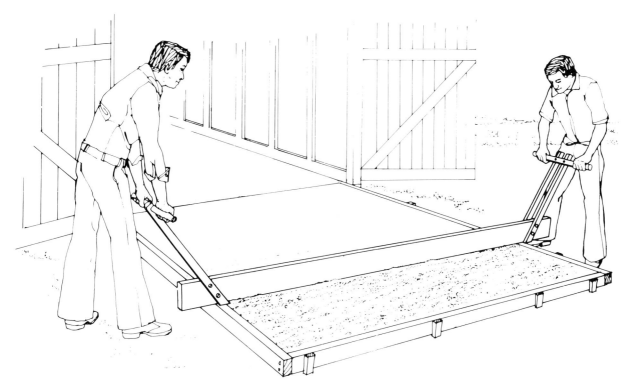

Tamping concrete

of the area to be paved with cords and stout stakes, checking that the angles are right-angles if the paving is to be rectangular. Drive in the long stakes along the line of the cords at 2′6″ (76cm) centres leaving 1′ (30cm) projecting and nail the boards to the inside. Check with the spirit level that the top edge has the right amount of slope. Where two boards join, provide additional support by nailing a stake at each board end. For curved edges, make a series of saw-cuts half way through the board to bend it round the curve—this will only work for a curve with a large radius.

Lay hardcore (or gravel) over the whole area as before, then lay 2″ (5cm) of sand and compact well. Pour concrete 1:2:4, spread it out with a shovel to a thickness of 4″ (10cm) and level off the top with the tamping board.

Drainage

If you cover the ground with any kind of paving material, you will greatly reduce the ability of the soil to absorb water. The sand bedding method will allow the water to drain away into the subsoil as long as sand is used in the jointing. The concrete and hardcore (or gravel) method, however, will require a gradient (grade) to enable rainwater to run off into the soil or to a rubble-filled trench placed at the lowest edge. The gradient (grade) or fall should be in one direction (away from the house) and about $1\frac{1}{2}''$ (3.5cm) to 10′ (3m).

Set long stakes 5′ (1.5m) apart and, with the aid of a 10′ (3m) long piece of wood 1″×6″ (2.5cm × 15cm) (our straight edge) and the spirit level, adjust them until they are all perfectly level. Then make a mark $1\frac{1}{2}''$ (3.7cm) from ground level on the stake at the desired lowest part of the gradient (grade) and hammer it further into the ground up to the mark. Now sink the intermediate

stake and sight them across until the tops of all the stakes are in line. Check with the straight edge. Now you can make the necessary adjustment in soil level.

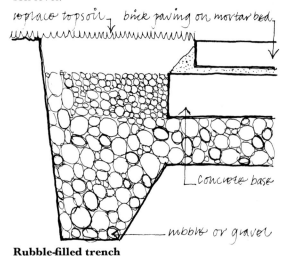

Rubble-filled trench

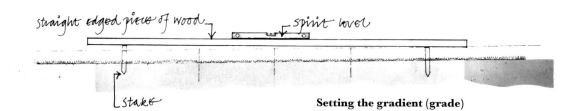

Setting the gradient (grade)

A Terrace can create an extra living area off a sitting room

64

Laying your bricks

The method of laying will depend on which bond pattern you have chosen. On the next few pages we illustrate some of the traditional ways of creating patterns with some hints about where they are most effective and in what circumstances.

For laying on a sand bed, lay the bricks in the pattern you have chosen, tapping each one into place and working it down level. Since the bricks will settle, it is a good idea to set them a little high. Start working from the middle of one side and lay a ribbon of your pattern all the way across the area in whatever direction you wish to go. Work from this middle ribbon towards each side. Try and leave a regular $\frac{3}{8}''$ (1cm) joint between bricks. As you get near the edges, tighten or loosen the joints as necessary so that you end with whole bricks whenever possible. Some patterns will require more brick-cutting than others and hints about this are given on the following pages.

Where bricks are to be laid on a concrete base they should be bedded in mortar using a 1:1:6 mix. Spread $\frac{1}{2}''$ (1.2cm) mortar on the concrete, place the bricks and tap into place. In other respects the laying is similar to laying on a sand bed described above. Check constantly with the straight edge to ensure an even surface.

Jointing

When the bricks are down to your satisfaction, you can start jointing.

Sand jointing. This is the easiest method. It can be either sand or a mixture of sand and earth. Brush this into the joints. Use a piece of wood to tamp the sand into the joints and allow it to settle over several days and repeat the process to bring the sand up to the top of the bricks. This method will encourage the rapid growth of moss and lichens which look very attractive. Weeds will grow as well and will have to be removed by hand if you do not wish to rid the path of the attractive lichens and moss by using a weed killer.

Dry mortar jointing. Alternatively, for a stronger joint and for bricks bedded in mortar on a concrete base, a mixture of cement and sand can be used. Mix this in the proportion of 1:6 and brush into the joints. Water with a fine spray from a garden watering-can or garden hose. Repeat this watering the next day to ensure the proper 'curing' of the mortar.

This method may cause staining on the surface of the bricks, so careful brushing is essential. If staining does occur, the only remedy is hard work, on hands and knees. Brush with a weak solution of muriatic acid and a stiff brush. Be sure to wear protective gloves.

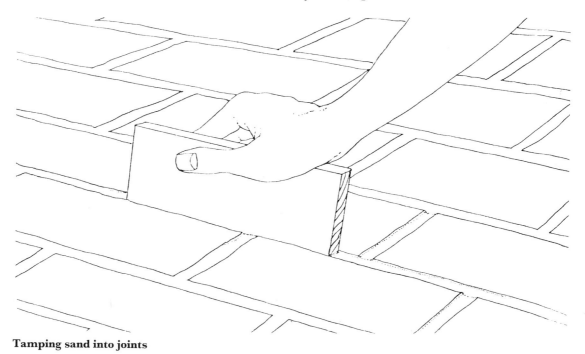

Tamping sand into joints

Running bond

This is one of the simplest patterns to lay. It is a directional pattern and as such can be used to very good effect leading up to a feature of the garden, a statue for instance, or as seen here running through sliding doors. How effectively it unites the inside and the outside. It is also a very good pattern to use for narrow paths where there is not room enough to make a large pattern work.

Of course running bond can be laid non-directionally for patios and terraces within defined areas. It doesn't require any major brick-cutting and looks very good edged with stack bond (jack-on-jack). If you are using a basket-weave or herringbone pattern over a large area, you can use running bond to break up the main pattern and superimpose a smaller scale. This can look most attractive for really large areas.

Your bricks can be laid either on edge or flat, the latter being the most economical of course. Running bond is very often used to aid drainage from a patio or terrace with water flowing in the direction of the joints.

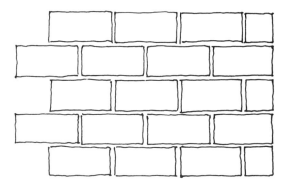

Running bond laid flat

Directional running bond used to unite reception area and courtyard in a commercial building in Dublin, Ireland.

Stack bond

This is a very simple pattern to lay and requires practically no cutting. It can look effective as seen here with sand in the joints and the bricks closely butted together. It is rather difficult to follow through a large area and still keep the regularity of the pattern.

It looks especially good in combination with running bond and just about anywhere where an edging is required.

Use several brick colours to brighten up the basic simplicity of the pattern and use the same bricks to follow through any structure like this barbecue which will be standing on it.

It is excellent for small patios and in town gardens.

Stack bond (jack-on-jack) laid flat

Stack bond barbecue area—pink and yellow bricks are used for both paving and barbecue. The barbecue is built without mortar in the joints, so it can be dismantled very easily.

Herringbone

Over many centuries, herringbone has proved one of the most popular paving patterns of all. It is a completely natural way to lay small units. It gives a secure interlocking pattern which is not static but has a certain movement in it as well. The reason for herringbone's popularity is because it is never tedious; from whichever direction you look at it, a different regularity of pattern results—either strong rows or zigzags. Bricks can be used on edge or flat and it is just as popular for indoor use. It looks good anywhere—on a narrow path or a large terrace. It is such a solid and secure pattern that it can be used successfully for roads carrying heavy urban traffic. A herringbone pattern will necessitate a lot of brick-cutting at the edges and could be edged with a row of running bond.

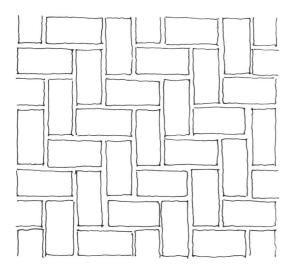

Herringbone laid flat

Greenish brick laid in a herringbone pattern adds to the intimate feeling of this North London mews.

Far right: Elegant herringbone paving in the courtyard of the Ducal Palace, Urbino, Italy.

Basketweave

This is a very adaptable pattern which gives many variations on a single theme. It gives a good interlocking 'static' pattern and would be used to best effect for a terrace or patio rather than a narrow path or walkway. It can be very effective in small patches broken up with concrete or bands of running or stack bond (jack-on-jack). It might be tricky, if you are paving a large area of terrace, to get the pattern right first time, so if you are laying a basketweave on a concrete base, set the bricks dry first to get the hang of it. Bricks can be laid flat or on edge or in a combination of both.

Basketweave on edge with cut bricks

Basketweave on edge

Brick laid flat in basketweave pattern with wide mortar joints.

Circular paving

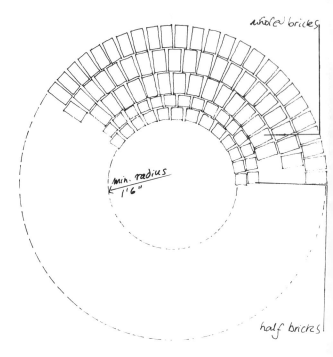

A circular paving pattern can be one of the most satisfying to the eye with its restful radiating lines and ever-increasing circles. They are used to their maximum potential in small areas, surrounding a tree, statue, birdbath or some other favourite garden object to create an instant focal point in the garden. If you lay a circular pattern on a sand bed with sand in the joints around a young tree there will be no problem at all when the tree thickens out. You can just remove the inner ring, with absolutely no damage to the roots of the tree.

Laying a circular pattern is not as difficult as most people think but the visual appeal of the pattern will be affected by the radius of your circle in relation to the length of your brick. With a small radius the outer ends of wedge-shaped joints can look rather unpleasant if they become very wide. It is a good idea to start the circles with half bricks and then change to full bricks as the radius increases.

Below: Rings of half-bricks in a circular pattern make an elegant setting for this stone garden statue.

Right: A modern brick planter is accentuated by a circular pattern.

Unusual effects and edging

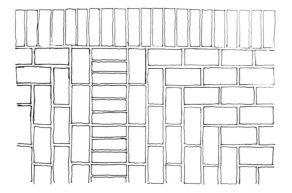

Running bond pattern with stack bond edging

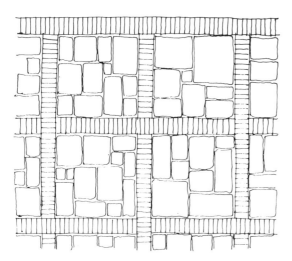

Bricks on edge with alternative infill for large scale pattern

Above: Old paving laid about 1875. The edge treatment allows spreading plants to encroach a certain distance onto the path without interrupting the main pattern.

Opposite right: Running bond pattern with stack bond (jack-on-jack) edging.

Opposite left: This intricate 19th-century shell-like paving pattern could be achieved today with a rough-textured brick and a lot of time and patience.

Planters

There has never been a more popular time for growing plants in every situation—gardens, large or small, tiny courtyards, small terraces and patios, atriums and conservatories, offices and miniature parks all over our cities.

No matter whether you own large expanses of green lawn, an unruly patch or a paved city garden, you may like to provide a container for your plants for ease of maintenance. Brick containers can be easy to build, attractive and functional— since the soil inside can be varied as required, and they can give an opportunity to create a kind of living sculpture with different shapes and textures. Of course, apartment floors and balconies are not suitable for the larger brick planters; here it's best to stick to some kind of plastic unit which will not add too much weight to the floor. But anyone on the ground level will find that bricks add so much texture and tone to the plants that the result is almost always easy to maintain, and delightful to look at.

As always, remember to keep a sense of proportion; if you want to grow a clump of white-stemmed birches in a planter, then it must be sufficiently tall and sufficiently wide to look stable. And the reverse is also true—a large planter would look pretty silly with a topping of 6″ pansies.

A multiple unit, with brick planters of different heights and widths, could look most attractive. This kind of arrangement would add enormously to the overall visual appeal, allowing you to grow plants that need different kinds of soil.

If you are a keen hydroponic gardener, then the same planters can be used, except that you will have to adapt them slightly—they won't need holes for continuous drainage but will need some means of allowing the water to escape when you wish to change the liquid nourishment.

Square planter

We have designed three bold and dramatic planters. Either singly or grouped together at different heights, they will make a strong focal point in your garden.

The square and circular planters are simple to build, using easily available standard bricks. The ornate hexagonal planter requires the use of standard 'specials'. The 'specials' may be slightly more difficult to obtain as these days they are usually made to order. Some legwork around a specialist brick merchant's yard may uncover a supply ordered by someone else, but not used, which will be quite sufficient for this project.

In other respects, the choice of brick is very wide. Generally, however, you will get the most satisfying results by using bricks similar to those described for paving and retaining walls (see pages 59 and 47). Briefly, the bricks should be 'hard-burnt'; avoid 'soft' and 'under-burnt' bricks unless the inside of the planter is lined with an impervious material such as polythene. The reason for this is that the brickwork will be wet or at least damp most of the time with no chance of drying out, and may deteriorate quickly, particularly in freezing conditions. For the 'complete look' build your planters on brick paving and use the same bricks for both paving and planters.

Since these planters are rather large and imposing they will look best built outside on a brick-paved terrace or patio, but if you have a really large room or entrance hall where a large free-standing object would not look out of place, they can add drama to an interior scheme. It is very important to remember that when full of damp earth all planters are very heavy and should only ever be built on a solid concrete floor. For interior use the insides should be lined with heavy duty polythene to contain the water.

Refer to indoor gardening manuals for details of suitable soil mixtures and drainage needed for plants. Outside, of course, the base should be left open for natural drainage.

This planter measures $5\frac{1}{2}$ bricks long by $5\frac{1}{2}$ bricks wide and it will be approximately 2′ (60cm) high.

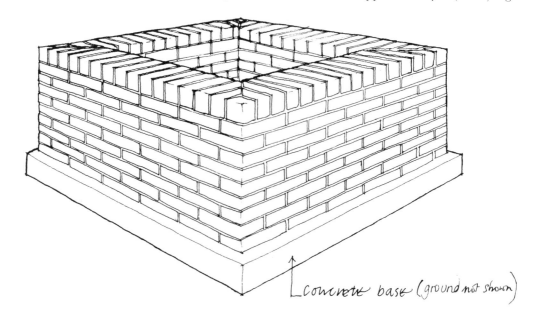

concrete base (ground not shown)

Tools
You will need all the basic tools listed on page 25 plus:
Right-angle square
Steel tape-measure
Gauge rod

Materials
You should use standard-sized solid bricks.
500 facing bricks
$\frac{1}{2}$ cu yd (0.35m³) concrete   1:2:4 mix
Mortar (see estimating table)   1:1:6 mix

Foundations

Excavate the ground for the base to the brickwork to form a trench approximately 1′ (30cm) wide × 1′ (30cm) deep, square on plan to the dimensions shown in fig. 2. Mix the concrete 1:2:4 and lay this in the trench to a depth of 6″ (15cm) and tamp with the edge of a board.

Because there is a very light load on the concrete in this case, a foundation is simply to form a sound, level base for the brickwork. There is no need to lay a slab, and the untouched soil within the square will act as drainage.

Brickwork

Spread mortar on the concrete strip and mark out a square for the inside dimension of the planter $3\frac{1}{2}$ bricks × $3\frac{1}{2}$ bricks.

Using the right-angle square begin with the corner brickwork and then continue laying nine courses as stretcher (running) bond in two half-brick skins (wythes) (fig. 3). Use the gauge rod to ensure even coursing. As the wall is only about 2′ (60cm) high, the overlapping arrangement of bricks laid in alternate courses at the corners (fig. 4) will provide sufficient bonding without it being necessary to bond the two skins together. The coping course will also be bonded, and will add to the wall's strength.

Remember to build up the corners of the planter first using the spirit level to check that the sides are vertical and the right-angle square to check right-angles. Bed the bricks well in mortar. Cut off surplus mortar with the trowel blade and try to avoid smearing the face of the bricks. Strike a flush joint as the mortar begins to set.

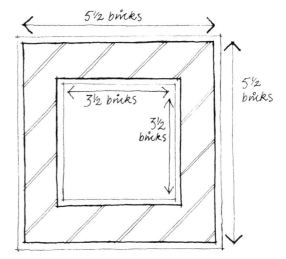

Fig. 2   Plan

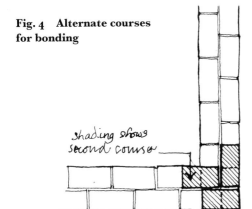

Fig. 4   Alternate courses for bonding

shading shows second course

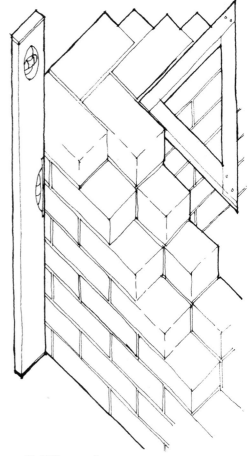

Fig. 3   Building up the corner

Coping

Construct this as a brick-on-edge (rowlock) coping. Lay each brick on edge across the thickness of the wall and bed each one solidly against the next. The corner coping bricks can either be mitre cut or straight butted bricks (fig. 5).

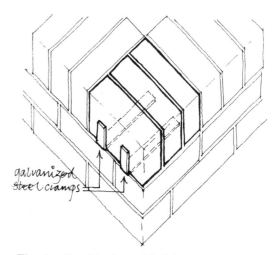

galvanized
steel clamps

Fig. 5b   Straight butted bricks

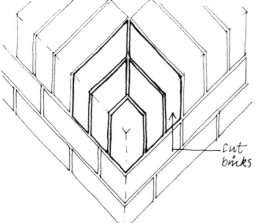

cut
bricks

Fig. 5a   Mitred corner

Another idea for a planter, this time using projecting specially shaped brick units. Both planter and adjacent wall have been designed to complement each other to the last detail.

Circular planter

This circular planter is basically similar in construction to the square one. The foundation is formed in exactly the same way except that it is circular instead of square.

A cylindrical form 3′ (90cm) high and 2′6″ to 3′ (76cm to 90cm) wide will simplify the task of accurately laying the bricks in a circle. Make this from a sheet of hardboard 3′×8′ (90cm × 2.5m) and bend it to form a cylinder. Tie strong string around it at the top, bottom and centre to keep it in shape.

Alternatively, you could use an oil drum or refuse bin of about 2′6″ to 3′ (76cm to 90cm) in diameter; it is only temporary and will be removed before the coping is laid.

Theoretically you have a wide choice of facing bricks for the project although the single-bullnose bricks will restrict your choice in fact. If you find bullnose bricks too expensive or too difficult to buy, use ordinary solid bricks. Because the planter will be in contact with wet earth, choose a brick with low water-absorption properties.

Tools
You will need all the basic tools listed on page 25 plus: $\frac{3}{8}$″ (1cm) diameter bent steel tube for shaping joints.

Materials
You should use standard-sized solid bricks.
350 facing bricks
150 single-bullnose bricks (or ordinary bricks)
$\frac{1}{2}$ cu yd (0.35m³) concrete   1:2:4 mix
Mortar (see estimating table)   1:1:6 mix
Hardboard 3′×8′ (90cm × 2.5m)

Foundations
Dig a circular trench about 1′ (30cm) wide × 1′3″ (38cm) deep; it need only be roughly circular, with an inside diameter of about 2′ (60cm).

Drive stout stakes in the trench bottom projecting 6″ (15cm). Make sure the tops are level using the spirit level and straight edge. Mix the concrete 1:2:4 and pour into the trench up to the top of the stakes. Tamp with the edge of a 4″×11″ (10cm × 28cm) board.

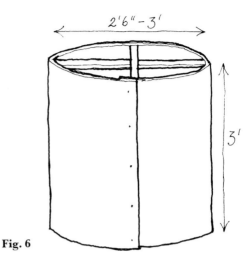

Fig. 6

Place the temporary form on the concrete base and check with the spirit level that it is vertical; if necessary, pack pieces of broken brick or tile under the edge until it stands straight.

Brickwork
When you have positioned the temporary form, set out a row of facing bricks on end (soldiers) with narrow face to the pipe, laying them without using mortar in order to gauge the joints (fig. 7). Keep the joint space at the back fairly narrow to avoid overwide and unsightly joints on the face (fig. 8). You may have to adjust them to get the bricks to fit around the form neatly without finishing up with a space too small for a brick but too wide for a joint. When you have established the spacing, bed the bricks in $\frac{1}{2}$″ (1.2cm) mortar spread on the concrete base and repeat this process dry for an outer row of bricks. Then lay these bricks in mortar, buttering the back and one side of each brick. It is important that the course of bricks (inner and outer rings) below ground should be one full course in order that, for the visual appeal of the planter, the first course (inner and outer rings) above ground is seen as a full course of bricks. To achieve this, you may have to lay a thicker mortar bed for the course below ground to bring the tops up to finished ground level.

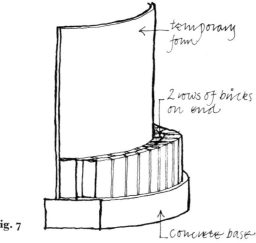

Fig. 7

Try to avoid air pockets in the mortar. Joint the bricks just laid with a slightly recessed joint. The finished look is not vital for this below-ground course, but doing it properly will serve as a useful exercise for gauging the spacing of subsequent courses.

Build up two inner and outer rows of bricks on end (soldiers) for each of the next two courses, staggering the long vertical joints in the outer row to occur over the centre of the brick below. Check each course with the spirit level to make sure that it is reasonably level. Now lay the final soldier course as before with an inner ring of bricks but use the single bullnose bricks for the outer row (fig. 9).

Fig. 8

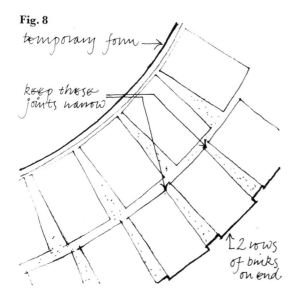

Jointing

Joint the brickwork above ground with a slightly recessed joint. Any variation in width which may occur will be less apparent with this kind of jointing. Use a piece of round steel bar $\frac{3}{8}''$ (1cm) in diameter, bent at an angle, to shape the joints.

Allow the mortar to harden for three to four days and remove the temporary form.

Check across the top with the spirit level, if any small adjustment is necessary this can be made by slightly increasing the thickness of the mortar.

Coping

You will need approximately 48 bullnose bricks for the coping. You will have to cut them using the brick set, hammer and gauge board described on page 26. Do this as carefully as possible, as the cut inside edge will also show. Measure the distance from the inside face of the top course of bricks to the point where the bullnose curve begins (fig. 9).

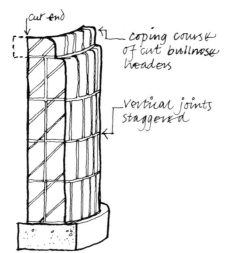

**Fig. 9
Section**

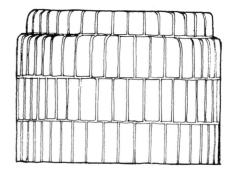

Side view of finished planter

This will be about 6½" (16cm). Measure this off on the bricks and cut them to this size (do not cut the bullnose off, of course!).

Now lay the coping course of cut bullnose bricks. Since they will be set back from the other brickwork, the diameter of this row will be smaller and it is a good idea to set them out dry first before bedding in mortar, to ensure correct joint spacing.

Variations on the same theme

Circular planters of varying heights and diameters grouped together can make an attractive feature. The very tall planters can be filled with trailing plants which will cascade down the sides. Most planters up to around 5′ (1.5m) high can be built around a removable circular form.

A grouped scheme such as this would look very attractive used in conjunction with the circular brick paving illustrated on pages 74-5. For maximum effect, use the same brick for both paving and planter.

Hexagonal planter

This ornate six-sided planter with a strong Victorian influence could almost qualify as a 'folly'. It is an extravaganza which should be embarked on only after very careful consideration.

It will need space around it and everything else such as terraces, steps, etc. should be generously proportioned. If you are fortunate enough to have a large Victorian conservatory attached to the house it would make a splendid centrepiece.

An appropriate choice of brick would be either smooth-faced red or cream. A greenish-glazed brick would be absolutely ideal.

It is quite a difficult project and requires a number of special bricks in small quantities. We call these plinth stretchers, plinth headers and single-cant facing bricks; if these terms are not used in your area, take the drawings along to your brick merchant. In addition, some of your special bricks will have to be cut to form the corners for each course. If possible have the bricks cut by a builder or stone mason with the right equipment because the amount of cutting is large in proportion to the project. Ask a good brick merchant for his advice and help.

Tools
You will need all the basic tools listed on page 25 plus:
Right-angle square
Steel tape-measure
Gauge rod
Bat-and-closer gauge

Materials
You should use standard-size solid bricks.

500 plain facing bricks
150 single-cant facing bricks
200 plinth stretchers
50 plinth headers
$\frac{1}{2}$ cu yd (0.35m³) concrete   1:2:4 mix
Mortar (see estimating table)   1:1:6 mix

Some of your bricks have to be cut as shown in fig. 12. In each case the angle will be 30°. The cutting schedule is:

12 mitred single-cant facing bricks (for brick-on-edge coping)	I
12 mitred single-cant facing bricks	II
12 mitred plinth stretchers ($\frac{1}{2}$ brick)	III
6 mitred plinth stretchers ($\frac{1}{2}$ brick)	IIIa
12 mitred plinth stretchers (full brick)	IV
6 mitred plinth stretchers (full bricks)	IVa
42 mitred facing bricks ($\frac{1}{2}$ brick)	V
42 mitred facing bricks (full brick)	VI
12 mitred brick-on-edge facing bricks	VII
12 mitred brick-on-edge facing bricks	VIII
$\frac{1}{2}''$ (1.2cm) plywood 6 rectangles 2'9" × 2'6" (82.5cm × 75cm)	

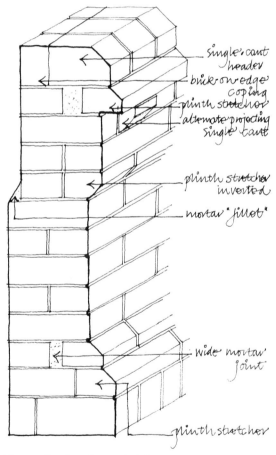

single-cant header
brick-on-edge coping
plinth stretcher
alternate projecting single-cant

plinth stretcher inverted

mortar "fillet"

wide mortar joint

plinth stretcher

Fig. 11   Section through side

86

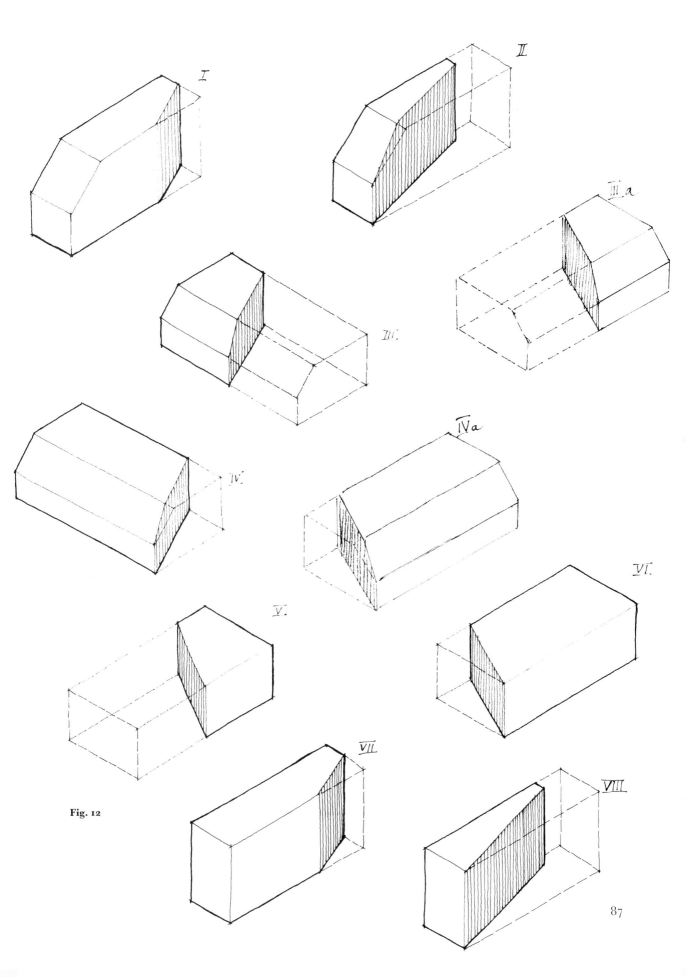

Fig. 12

87

Foundations

Before starting work, we suggest that, to achieve the hexagon, you should construct a temporary plywood form around which to build the brickwork. Use $\frac{1}{2}''$ (1.2cm) plywood. Cut six pieces each $2'9''$ (82.5cm) long × $2'6''$ (75cm) high and nail battens across to form a hexagon (fig. 13).

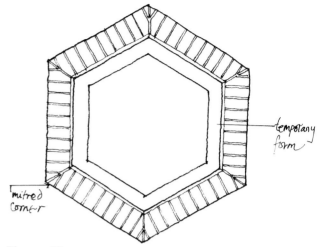

Fig. 14   Plan

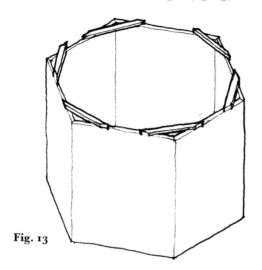

Fig. 13

Using the hexagonal form to establish the position on the ground, excavate the trench for the concrete footing approximately $1'3''$ (38cm) wide × $1'$ (30cm) deep. Lay 6" (15cm) of concrete for the foundation; make sure it is level by means of the spirit level, and a straight edge laid across stakes (see page 32).

Position the plywood form on the concrete base and lay two courses of one-brick-thick brickwork in stretcher (running) bond around it. These courses will be below ground or paving level and can be quite rough brickwork; they should, of course, be level, as future courses will be laid on top. There is no brick cutting required for this below-ground course—spaces can be filled with mortar.

The brickwork above ground

First course. Lay an inner brick-on-edge course close up to the form, and fill the intersection at the angle with mortar (fig. 15). Then, using the mitred header bricks VII and VIII, form the first corner, bedding each cut brick carefully in mortar and tapping into position. Lay each corner in the same

way and then for the rest of the course lay the bricks as headers on edge. Lay them dry first between the corners to gauge the required joint width and then lay them in mortar.

Second course. For the second course above ground, lay a rough header backing course flat and, on the face, plinth stretchers starting at each corner and working out (fig. 16). At the corners lay mitred bricks III and IV.

Third Course. Lay the third course above ground in a similar way but lay the backing course as stretchers. Make sure all the spaces are well filled with mortar. At the corner lay mitred bricks IIIa and IVa.

Fourth to eighth course. Continue with five course of one-brick-thick brickwork laid stretcher (running) bond. At the corners lay mitred bricks VII and VIII.

Ninth course For the ninth course lay the plinth stretchers inverted and set forward so that the splay coincides with the brick face below (fig. 11). At the corners lay mitred bricks III and IV.

Tenth course. Lay the next course stretcher (running) bond again. At the corners lay mitred bricks VII and VIII.

Eleventh course. Next, starting from each corner, lay mitred headers VII and VIII. On each side of the corner bricks lay an inverted single cant laid forward from the brickwork below by the extent of the splay. These projecting bricks are known as dentils; and here they alternate with plain headers set back to the face (fig. 17).

Twelfth course. For the last course but one, lay plinth stretchers on the face with a stretcher backing course and fill the space between with mortar (fig. 11). At the corners lay mitred bricks III and IV.

Thirteenth course. Finally, lay the coping course of single cant headers, at the corners lay mitred bricks I and II and when the mortar has fully set, say after six to seven days, carefully remove the plywood form (fig. 18).

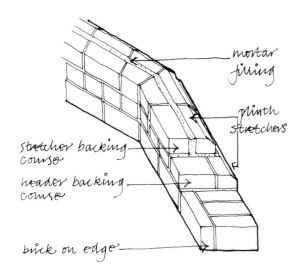

inner brick on edge close up to form

angle filled with mortar

header on edge

Fig. 15   First course

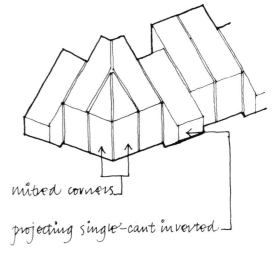

mitred corners

projecting single-cant inverted

Fig. 17   Eleventh course

mortar filling

plinth stretchers

stretcher backing course

header backing course

brick on edge

Fig.16   First, second and third courses

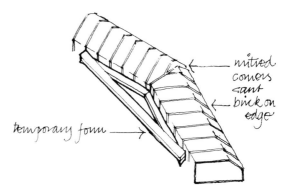

mitred corners cant brick on edge

temporary form

Fig. 18   Coping

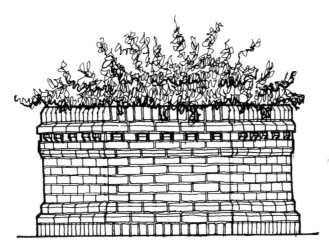

Garden furniture

Our love of order and arrangement does not confine itself to indoor living space. Outdoors we like to see well-kept carpets of grass, carefully trimmed herbaceous borders, evenly spaced trees and regular vegetable patches. But gardens are also places for relaxation and recreation, and in this repect we demand as great a degree of comfort outdoors as we expect indoors: to most of us a well-furnished garden is as desirable as a well-furnished house.

The most elegant and time-tested way of furnishing a garden is to make a feature of the sitting area, to make it a permanent part of the garden landscape, whether a bench seat under shady oaks, a curved seat and a table to fit into a secluded nook, or comfortable chairs and low tables taking pride of place on a patio or terrace, or around a pool.

The material chosen to make garden seats and tables has always been dictated by the climate and by materials available locally—marble is much used in southern European regions. Italy, for example, boasts many fine marble seats dating from as long ago as the Renaissance, embellished with fine carvings; but in colder climates a marble slab, no matter how elegantly decorated, would lose its appeal. Wooden seats and tables, while attractive for their natural quality, suffer in rainy climates. Our brick table and seating would be at home anywhere in the world.

We have recommended mosaic tiles for both the top of the table and seating units, but for extra comfort cushions can be put on top of the seat. At the end of the summer or on a rainy day, only the cushions will have to be brought indoors.

In all other respects, our garden furniture would be quite permanent, withstanding any kind of bad weather. It would look especially good on a patio or terrace—like a bold piece of sculpture. We have designed the seating unit so that plants and trees can be grown inside the curves.

Getting started

A very useful extension of your living space can be created by making more of the patio. Brick paving will provide an outdoor 'room' which can be used for most of the year; it can be extended by building a table and seating unit in brick—permanent outdoor furniture whose sculptural quality will give visual interest even when not being used.

Almost any kind of facing bricks can be used for this project; the most suitable are frost-resistant, i.e. reasonably hard-burnt. As a contrast with the smooth texture of the top of the table and seating, a rough, slightly irregular-shaped brick would look good. If you decide to lay a brick patio at the same time, use the same kind of brick for both furniture and patio.

In addition to the facing bricks, $1\frac{1}{4}''$ paving bricks or quarry tiles are needed for the edging to the table, and single-bullnose bricks for the seating. You will find that paving bricks are available in dark tones of brown and blue brown, and quarry tiles (which are similar but thinner) come in these colours as well as lighter browns: russet brown and golden brown. Choose these carefully to suit the facing bricks. As there will be almost as much mortar as paver showing on the edging, we suggest that the mortar for the edging should be mixed with coloured cement to match them. If possible, the sand used in the mix should be darker than normal. Mix small amounts to try various combinations before making a final decision. Remember, mortar lightens in colour as it dries.

For the top we suggest glass mosaics which are available in a wide colour range and because of their small size can fit into the curves without precision cutting. Naturally, tiles can be used instead and these are available in an infinite variety of colours, textures and patterns.

To make building the round table easier, we advise you to construct a circular wooden form in plywood similar to the one described for the circular planter on page 83 but this time with a diameter of 2′6″ (76cm) and a height of 2′ (30cm). Or you could use an empty oil drum or similar cylindrical container of the right diameter and height. Unlike in the planter project, this does not have to be removed.

Tools

You will need all the basic tools listed on page 25 plus:
Short stakes and 10′ (3m) long cord
Pointing trowel
Hawk
Wood float

Materials

You should use standard-sized solid bricks
1 cu yd (m³) concrete
1800 facing bricks
500 single-bullnose bricks (or ordinary bricks)
100 $1\frac{1}{4}''$ (30cm) paving bricks or quarry tiles
4 6′ × 3′6″ (1.8m × 1m) sheets of corrugated asbestos cement
Mortar (see estimating table) 1:1:6 mix
One bag of white cement for grouting
56 sheets 12″ × 12″ (30cm × 30cm) glass mosaics
1 sheet hardboard 4″ × 8″ (10cm × 20cm)

Seating: laying out and foundations

Strip off 6″ (15cm) of topsoil from the whole area. Now lay out the double curve for the seating which is not unlike a serpentine wall.

Decide on the position you wish the whole seating and table unit to occupy and drive a stout stake into the ground roughly in the centre of the table area—centrepoint A. Hammer a nail into the stake and attach the cord to this.

Measure off 5′ (1.5m) on the cord and attach a sharpened stick to the end to act as a marker. Mark

Fig. 1 Marking out a circle with sharpened stick and sand

Fig. 2   General plan of seating and table

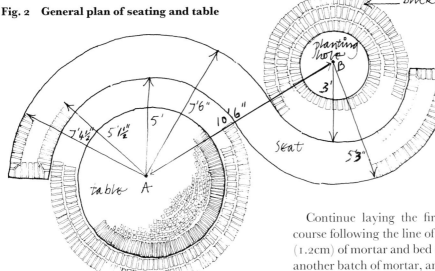

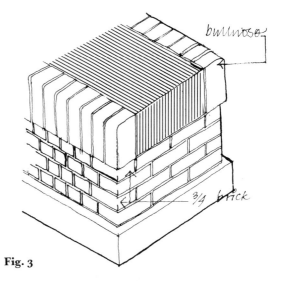

$\frac{1}{3}$ of a circle with the sharpened stick and run sand along this mark (fig. 1). Now measure off 7′6″ (2.3m) on the cord and mark the ground in the same way.

From a second centrepoint B positioned 10′6″ (3.2m) from A mark another $\frac{1}{3}$ of a circle, this time with radii 3′ (90cm) and 5′3″ (1.6m). You now have the inner and outer edges of the curved foundation for the seating.

Dig out between the sand lines to a depth of 6″ (15cm) and ram the trench bottom. Drive stout stakes at intervals of approximately 4′ (1m) into the trench bottom and level using the straight edge and spirit level. Adjust as necessary. Pour concrete 1:2:4 into the trench up to the top of the stakes and tamp across with the edge of a board.

Mix a batch of mortar 1:1:6 and lay $\frac{1}{2}$″ (1.2cm) on the concrete and, with the sharpened stick and cord, outline the curves of the seating again as a guide for the outside face of the brickwork only this time the measurements will be 5′1$\frac{1}{2}$″ (1.5m) and 7′4$\frac{1}{2}$″ (2.2m) from A, and 3′ (90cm) and 5′3″ (1.6m) from B.

Seating: brickwork

The brickwork for the seating will be laid as an outer and inner row. Each row will be laid as headers. The brickwork at the ends of the seat will be laid half-brick stretcher (running) bond and these ends should be built first (fig. 3).

Continue laying the first course as a header course following the line of the foundation. Lay $\frac{1}{2}$″ (1.2cm) of mortar and bed each brick on this. Mix another batch of mortar, and with the bricklayer's trowel, spread it about 3″ (7.5cm) thick on the first course of bricks. Bed the next course, tapping the bricks into the mortar with the trowel handle. Lay three courses of bricks, all headers, with three-quarter bats every alternate course at each end, following the curves established by the first course; check frequently with the spirit level to make sure that the courses are horizontal. Strike a flush joint as you go.

Now lay two courses of bricks on the inside edge of the top course as stretcher courses; set these back about $\frac{1}{2}$″ (1.2cm) in from the inside face (fig. 4). Lay two courses at each end but set these back 1″ (2.5cm) from the outside face of the brickwork, this will allow the mosaic finish on the ends to be flush with the brickwork.

Fig. 3

93

Seating: top

To form the top of the seating, cut the corrugated asbestos-cement sheeting in the direction of the corrugations in lengths of 1'6" (46cm), 1'6" (46cm) wide. Safety codes permit the cutting of asbestos-cement with a handsaw used in the open air. Bed these on a mortar bed on top of the inner brickwork. To get round the curves, each piece will slightly overlap the adjoining piece like a fan. Check with the spirit level that the top is level.

Now lay the bullnose bricks for the edging of the seating. Mix mortar and lay a bed with a good quantity at the back against the half-brick inner ring. The edging needs care to achieve smooth curves and a level top. The edging joints will be slightly wedge-shaped as the bricks follow the curve. The joints on the inside curve will be narrower than those on the outside curve and the narrowest should be about $\frac{1}{4}$" (6mm). When the mortar has set, but before it hardens, rake out the joints to a depth of about $\frac{1}{2}$" (1.2cm) using a piece of flat metal strip $\frac{1}{4}$" (6mm) wide. Mix a quantity of mortar 1:3 and lay this on the asbestos cement sheeting, spreading and working it into the edges, but try to avoid getting it on the brick edging. Level this mixture off with a wood float to finish $\frac{3}{4}$"

(2cm) below the top of the brickwork. Leave it to harden for two to three days.

Lay out the mosaics. These come on square paper sheets and are laid paper side uppermost. Mix cement and water until it has the consistency of thick cream and spread this slurry about $\frac{1}{8}$" (3mm) thick; then lay the mosaics on it. Fill in spaces and edges with single mosaics before the slurry sets. Single mosaics can be cut with a pair of pincers.

After a couple of days, soak off the paper with warm water and then finish off by mixing the white cement with water to a paste. Grout the mosaics with the cement, spreading it over the surface and working it into the joints. Clean off the surplus, wipe down with a damp cloth and polish when dry.

Finally, mix the coloured cement and coloured sand (1:4$\frac{1}{2}$) and point up the edging brick. Using the pointing trowel cut off the mortar to make a flush joint.

Fig. 4   Section through seating

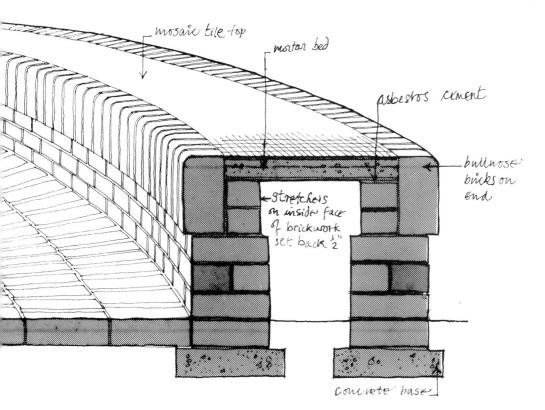

Table: laying out and foundations

The table is laid out in a very similar way to the seating.

Use the cord and sharpened stick attached to the stake in position A (fig. 2) and mark out a sand circle with a diameter of 4′ (1.2m). Excavate to a depth of 6″ (15cm) and ram the trench bottom. Drive in four equally spaced short stakes around the permieter to project 6″ above the trench bottom. Level these across with the spirit level and straight edge. Now lay the concrete to the top of the stakes and tamp with the edge of a board across the tops to make a level base.

Mix a batch of mortar and spread in a circle roughly 2′6″ (76cm) in diameter and about 2″ (5cm) thick. Place the temporary cylindrical form on this mortar bed, and check that it is level. Clean off any surplus mortar from the outside edge and spread a ½″ (1.2cm) bed around the form. Lay the first course of facing bricks as a header course, butting the bricks against the form.

Fig. 5   Section through table

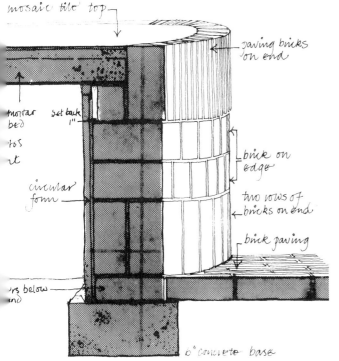

mosaic tile top

paving bricks on end

mortar bed to s t

set back 1″

brick on edge

circular form

two rows of bricks on end

brick paving

rs below nd

6″ concrete base

Table: brickwork above ground

Lay the next course as an inner ring of bricks on end (soldier course), with the narrow face against the circular form. Make sure that there is enough mortar between the bricks to fill the joints. Now repeat this as an outer ring, keeping the joints at the back as close as possible. Lay the next two courses as headers butting each up against the form.

For the top lay an inner ring of soldiers cut in half widthways and set back 1″ (2.5cm) from the inside face of the brickwork below. This half-brick-ring will provide the backing for the paving bricks or quarry tiles.

Table: top

Cut the corrugated asbestos in the same way as for the top of the seating; this time we need to cover a circle 3′3″ (99cm) in diameter and as the sheets normally come 2′6″ (76cm) wide, we will need to cut several sheets to fit. Bed the asbestos cement sheeting in mortar on the top of the inner brick-work.

Make the edging for the table with the paving bricks or quarry tiles laid on end. You will need a lot of mortar as the units are narrow and consequently there are more joints, so mix twice as much mortar as you have been using for the facing bricks. Use the coloured cement and coloured sand for a mortar similar in colour to the paving bricks.

Position a couple of bricks around the perimeter to provide temporary support for the thin paving bricks. Don't put mortar between the first paving brick and its temporary support but position them tightly butted up against each other. Of course, the first paving brick will have mortar at the back and base.

Spread a mortar bed on the top of the outer row of bricks and lay the paving bricks on end on this, tapping them into place. Lay about 1′ (30cm) at a time. Keep a ¼″ (6mm) joint at the back to avoid a very wide joint at the front. Strike off the mortar with the trowel edge to give a flush joint. Check frequently to make sure that the edging is level— you don't want a table that tilts! When the mortar has hardened, about three to four days, remove the temporary bricks and fill the spaces with paving bricks bedded in fresh mortar. Finish the top with mosaics laid in the same way as described for the seating.

Garden seat

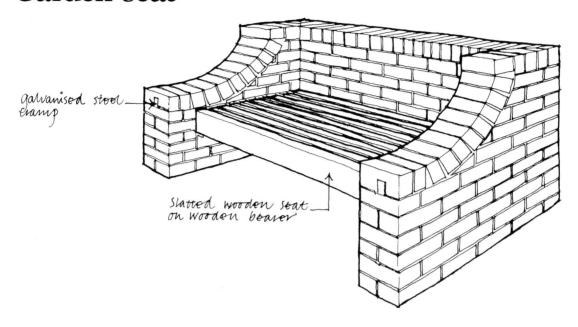

galvanised steel
cramp

Slatted wooden seat
on wooden bearer

Getting started

This super garden seat—a modern equivalent of
the traditional lion-headed stone garden seat—is
very easy to build and would be a useful and
handsome addition to any garden. If you have a
good view, position the seat to take full advantage
of it. Colourful cushions in brightly patterned
tough fabric filled with polyester foam chips will
add comfort and eye appeal

The seat is fairly easy to make but before you
begin, be sure to read about laying out, foundations (pages 29-31) and bricklaying (pages 34-
5).

The types of brick suitable are those with high
frost-resistant and low water-absorption properties. The bricks should have similar colour and
texture on all four faces as the seat will be seen from
all sides. Sand-faced facing bricks are unlikely to
be suitable.

A hardwood would be ideal for the timber slats.
Hardwoods are suitable for outdoor use without
preservative treatment. They look good and since
they are dense and close-grained, will not absorb
water or splinter like softwoods—an obvious advantage where seating is concerned!

Tools

You will need all the basic tools listed on page 25 plus:
Right-angle square
Line and pins (or nails)
$\frac{3}{8}''$ (1cm) diameter bent steel rod for shaping joints.

Materials

You should use standard-sized solid bricks.
300 facing bricks
$\frac{1}{2}$ cu yd (0.35m³) concrete   1:2:4: mix
Mortar (see estimating table)   1:1:6 mix
10 lengths hardwood 2″ × 4″ (5cm × 10cm)
approximately 6′ (1.8m) long.
2 steel bearers 3″ × 3″ (7.5cm × 7.5cm) 2′ (60cm) long
2 galvanized steel cramps 9″ × $\frac{3}{4}''$ × $\frac{1}{8}''$
(23cm × 2cm × 3mm)

Laying out and foundations

Decide on the position and the rough size and strip off the top soil, say around 6″ (15cm). Lay out the area with cord and stout stakes and excavate to a further depth of 6″ (15cm). Tamp the bottom of the trench and drive in four stout wooden stakes to protrude 6″ (15cm) above the trench bottom. Make sure the tops of the stakes are level by means of the spirit level and straight edge (see page 31).

Mix the concrete 1:1:6 and pour it into the trench up to the top of the stakes and tamp the surface across with the edge of a 2″ × 4″ (5cm × 10cm) board.

Brickwork

Mix some mortar and spread it $\frac{1}{2}$″ (1.2cm) thick on the concrete base. With the point of the trowel and the right-angle square, mark the outside edge of the brickwork. Lay the bricks in stretcher (running) bond in two skins, building up the corners first and working outwards in the usual way. Lay seven courses or the number nearest equivalent to 1′9″ (52.5cm) if you are using a brick thinner than $2\frac{5}{8}$″.

Now, still working from the outside, continue building up the back part of the wall another six courses, or the nearest number of courses to 1′6″ (45cm), to form the back of the seat.

To form the curve for each arm you will have to cut the horizontal bricks to a rake (fig. 7) following the line of the curve. Cut these bricks and position them. Now lay the brick-on-edge (rowlock) coping starting from each end of the arms, and building in a galvanized steel cramp to keep the first brick in position. Corner bricks can be either mitre cut or straight butted.

Slightly rake out the mortar joints and shape them with a $\frac{3}{8}$″ (1cm) diameter bent steel rod.

After fourteen days, when the mortar has hardened sufficiently, drill holes in the steel angle—three for fixing to the brickwork and ten for fixing the hardwood slats. Screw the steel angle bearers to the plugs at each end of the seat (fig. 7). Finish by positioning the slats in the angle bearers and fixing them by screwing from beneath.

Fig. 7   Section

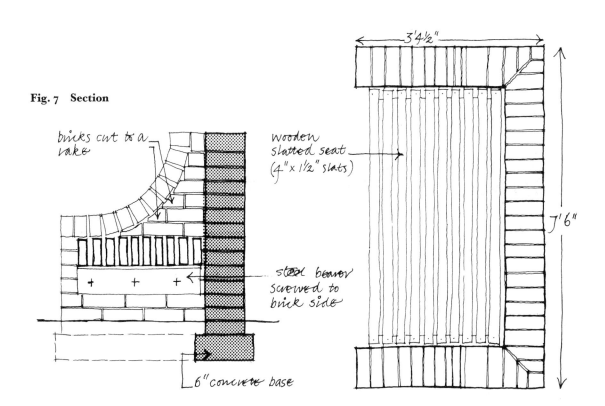

bricks cut to a rake

6″ concrete base

wooden slatted seat (4″ x 1½″ slats)

steel bearer screwed to brick side

3′4½″

1′6″

Barbecues

Sizzling steaks, sauced spare ribs, toasting forks filled with melting cheese and red tomatoes, marshmallows and baked potatoes, pan fried trout, all taste better and more exciting when cooked and eaten outdoors. During the last ten or twenty years, the barbecue has become apart of our lives; it is better than a picnic and more fun than a cold lunch packed in a hamper.

The principles of cooking over an open fire are few and simple. The fire box which holds the fuel must be high enough off the ground to allow a decent draft underneath, and deep enough to hold adequate fuel, wood or charcoal, so that after the flames have died down, enough heat is left to continue cooking the food. The grill should be big enough to hold a decent amount of food comfortably, without too much crowding. In spite of what the cookbooks and advertisements tell you, many cuts which taste best barbecued, such as thick chops and steaks, take a fiar amount of time, and the fun will be a bit less if half of you are gazing hungrily at the other half for twenty minutes or so. From these few basic requirements, the permutations are endless. We have given you three possibilities, the beginner's project for a small family that does not do too much outdoor cooking but wants somewhere to grill a few hot dogs and hamburgers during the summer parties for the children, or make baked potatoes when everyone gets together for leaf gathering in the autumn. The second is a permanent addition to your patio or terrace. The third is for the real barbecue convert who enjoys cooking outdoors and often invites guests for an evening barbecue and who has enough space to make and enjoy the elaborate seating.

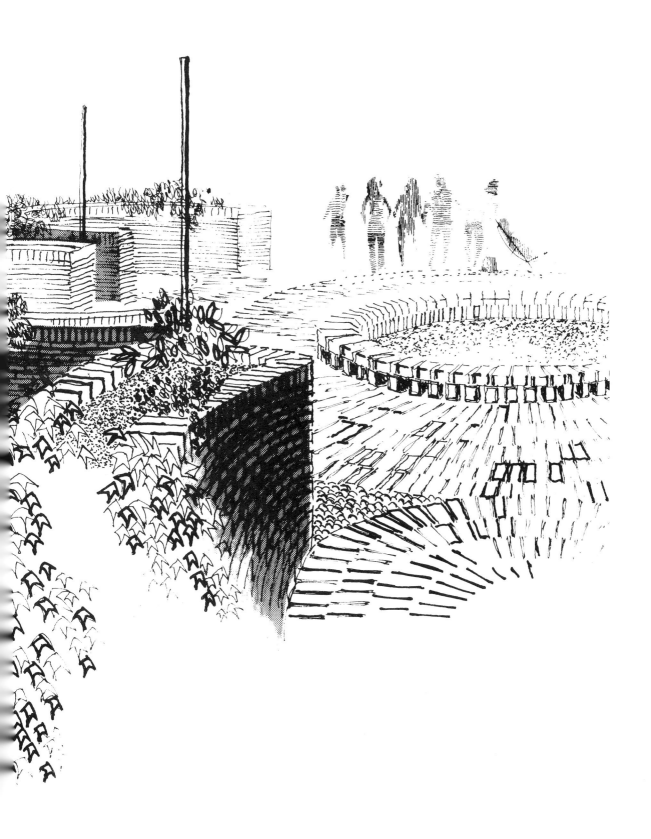

Beginner's barbecue

This is a very simple and cheap barbecue to put together; build it one morning and be using it that afternoon! You don't even need to mix mortar as the bricks are laid dry; simply arrange them as shown below—almost literally child's play.

Despite its simplicity, the barbecue is visually very attractive. We have arranged it with two handy tables for glasses, bottles etc. but if you are having a large party, two or three barbecues and several small tables can easily be assembled and then taken down again. You won't need to prepare foundations but take care to build on a paved terrace or very flat lawn to ensure that the barbecue won't overturn and spill hot charcoal over your guests.

Choose a brick which is regular in shape and preferably not perforated as the bricks nearest the heat may crack. A solid wirecut brick is ideal.

Tools

Spirit level
Broad-faced hammer
Brick set

Materials

250 regular-sized bricks
2 2′ × 2′ (60cm × 60cm) concrete paving slabs
1 sheet of perforated steel
1 grill

Building the barbecue

Decide on the site for your barbecue than lay the first and second courses of bricks in the arrangement shown in fig. 1a. Adjust the positions of the bricks as necessary until the spaces between bricks are roughly equal, measuring about $4\frac{1}{2}''$ (11.5cm) at the front edge of the first course.

Repeat this arrangement for subsequent courses; continue overlapping the bricks and leaving the same spaces as before. For the tables, build up nine courses and lay the 2′ × 2′ (60cm × 60cm) concrete paving slabs for the tops. For the bar-

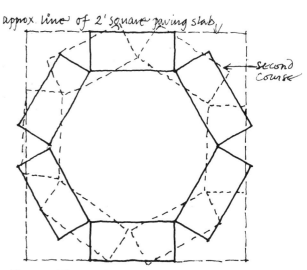

approx. line of 2′ square paving slab

second course

Fig. 1a First and second courses

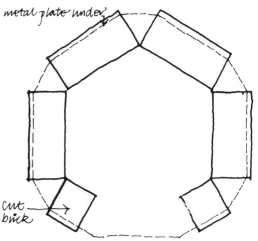

metal plate under

cut brick

Fig. 1b Penultimate course

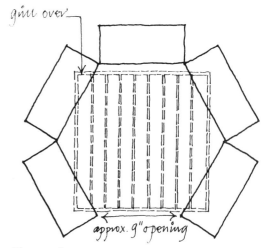

grill over

approx. 9″ opening

Fig. 1c Last course

becue, build up to the eleventh course and place a
perforated steel sheet on this course for the
charcoal.

Cut four bricks in half and position them at the
front as you can see in the photograph and fig. 1b,
and continue the brick ring. For the last course lay
another ring similar but without the half bricks,
and leave an opening at the front. Lay four bricks
in a square formation and position a grill on the
rim of the top course.

Check that the brickwork is vertical with the
spirit level as you lay the bricks.

*Simple-to-build barbecue designed by John Adams
(Ronald Adams Associates). The same design can be
adapted to create other ideas for your garden—flower
tubs of different heights and sizes, seats, bird-tables and
many other variations.*

Permanent barbecue

Although simple, the barbecue will look good as well as being very useful for Sunday lunch-time or entertaining on warm evenings. It is designed as four simply-built brick piers parallel to each other with a concrete slab at each side of the grill.

We recommend that you pave the area on either side of it with bricks of the same kind as you have chosen for the barbecue, laid stack bond (jack-on-jack) to match the piers; this is optional, of course.

Carefully chosen bricks will enhance the finished appearance. The bricks should have a good finish on both stretcher faces as both sides of the piers will be visible at the same time. You don't have to cut any bricks for the barbecue although minor brick-cutting may be necessary for the paving, so don't immediately be put off if the brick you like is very hard. We suggest you use a very regular brick with smooth faces, in conjunction with a flush or bucket-handle mortar joint. Coloured mortar may also look effective.

The 'table' slabs can be tiled with decorative patterned tiles; they should be frost-proof.

Tools
You will need all the basic tools listed on page 25 plus:
Right-angle square
Short stakes and cord
Gauge rod
$\frac{3}{8}''$ (1cm) diameter bent steel tube for shaping joints (optional)

Materials
You should use standard-sized solid bricks.
250 facing bricks for the barbecue
750 facing bricks suitable for paving
Mortar (see estimating table) 1:1:6 mix
$\frac{1}{6}$ cu yd (m³) concrete 1:2:4 mix
$\frac{1}{6}$ cu yd (m³) hardcore (or gravel)
2″ (5cm) thick pre-cast concrete paving slabs measuring 4′ × 1′ × 6″ (12cm × 30cm × 15cm)
2 sq yds (m²) decorative frost-proof tiles
Steel pan for the charcoal
Grill 2′8″ (80cm) square

Foundation slab
Prepare the ground where the barbecue is to be built—a rectangle 12′ wide (3.6m) × 15′ (4.6m) long. Excavate this area to a depth of 9″ (23cm) (fig. 3), checking with the spirit level, short stakes and straight edge that the excavated ground surface is level.

Using 1″ × 6″ (2.5cm × 15cm) boards, construct wooden forms for casting the concrete for the base. Lay out a rectangle 3′6″ (1m) wide × 9′ (27.4m) long in the centre of the excavated area with short stakes and cord. Drive 2″ × 2″ (5cm × 5cm) wooden stakes into the ground 3″ (7.5cm) in from each corner and along the line of the cords—five along each long side and three along each short side. Nail boards to the inside of the stakes so the bottom edge of each just touches the bottom of the excavated ground. Check with the spirit level that the boards are level.

Mix concrete 1:2:4 and pour into the forms to a

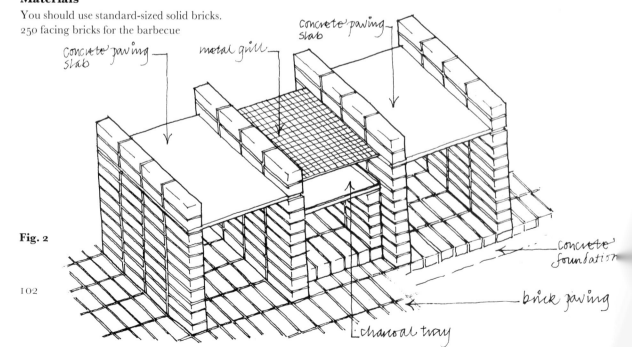

Fig. 2

concrete paving slab

metal grill

concrete paving slab

concrete foundation

brick paving

charcoal tray

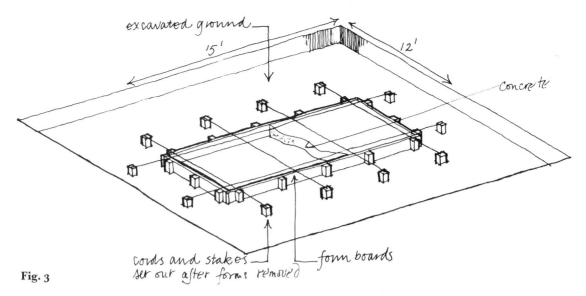

excavated ground

15'

12'

concrete

cords and stakes set out after forms removed

form boards

Fig. 3

depth of 6″ (15cm). With a straight-edged piece of wood, say 2″ × 4″ (5cm × 10cm), tamp off the concrete flush with the edges of the form boards.

When you have removed the forms, lay out four sets of cords and short stakes 2′10½″ (87.6cm) apart across the slab to serve as building lines for the piers (fig. 3), starting 2½″ (6cm) in from one end. Next set out two parallel cords 3′ (90cm) apart along the length of the slab and check that the cords are all at right-angles. Careful laying out is essential.

Lay hardcore (or gravel) 4″ (10cm) thick in the excavated area around the slab, ramming thoroughly to compact it. Face the hardcore (or gravel) with 2″ (5cm) of sand and lay the brick paving (see pages 56-77). We suggest you use the stack bond (jack-on-jack) pattern to match the piers. Fill the joints with dry sand.

Piers

Pick up a generous lump of mortar on the trowel and spread it on the concrete slab about 1½″ (3.7cm) thick. Bed the first course of bricks as stretchers in the mortar: fill the joints between each brick and tap gently into place with the trowel handle. Lay the next course directly over the first with vertical joints in line. This is not the usual way bricks should be laid—most brickwork should be bonded in one of the traditional methods for strength—but it will be sufficient for this project and give a distinctive appearance.

Continue building up all four piers. Strike off the mortar as you go and after four courses, finish the jointing—either flush or bucket handle (see page 38). Continue in this way up to ten courses above

slab level for all four piers, checking as the bricks are laid, that the brickwork is vertical and that the tops of the piers are level. If you are using a brick thinner than 2⅝″ (7.5cm) build up the nearest number of courses 2′6″ (75cm). Always check with the gauge rod.

Slab shelves

If your pre-cast concrete slabs for the shelves either side of the grill do not measure 3′ wide, you will have to cut them to fit. Measure the correct width and mark with a wax crayon. Cut a groove with the broad-faced hammer and brick set, using quick, sharp blows. Put a straight piece of wood under the line of the cut and break off the unwanted part with a sharp blow.

Spread 1½″ (3.5cm) mortar on the top of the 1½″ (3.5cm) of brickwork each side of the ends of the slab so clean off the surface mortar from this. Complete the brickwork by adding two more courses to each pier and point the joints as before.

Grill and charcoal tray

It now remains to build up the inside of the middle section to form the support for the charcoal tray which will be approximately 2′3″ (68cm) deep from front to back. Lay seven courses from slab level on the inside face of the two centre piers.

Position the steel pan to hold the charcoal in between the two centre piers. Also position the grill, sliding it in between the centre piers level with the concrete slabs, and your barbecue is complete.

Fire-pit barbecue

This is a simple fire-pit barbecue; it has been designed in conjunction with low level curved walls which will double up as windbreaks and seating. Choose additional outdoor furniture which does not need much looking after – teak or aluminium, for instance; the aluminium reproductions of Victorian cast-iron furniture would be ideal. This is a much more permanent form of barbecue and will take longer to build, so time in considering the site will be well spent.

Before embarking on this project, check with your local fire-officer that the site you have chosen is allowable. Certainly you must do this if you intend to build near a fence or boundary line. Check also with your local building office.

When you have satisfied any local requirements, consider the position in relation to the house. If possible choose a location where house or existing walls can form a protective screen from the prevailing wind, or where the barbecue will catch the late afternoon and evening sun.

To add to the after-dark effect and the glow from the barbecue itself, we have designed the chairs with sockets to hold large wax garden flares which can be bought at most department stores.

A word of warning: if there are likely to be very small children around, adapt the fire-pit so that it clears the ground by about 2' (60cm) and make sure the garden flares are well out of reach or leave them out altogether.

The semi-circular seats are built in two brick skins so that plants can be grown in between. For the 'complete' look pave the area between the firepit and chairs around the edge with bricks in circular pattern.

This design is illustrated on page 99.

Tools

You will need all the basic tools listed on page 25 plus: Short stakes and 10' (3m) long cord

Materials

3500 facing bricks
300 hard-burnt bricks
150 plinth headers (or ordinary bricks)
1500 paving bricks—for paving
5 2'6" diameter circular concrete paving slabs
8 cu yds (6m³) rubble or gravel
2 cu yds (m³) sand for bedding the brick paving
2½ cu yds (m³) concrete 1:2:4 mix
4 7' (2.1m) lengths of 1½" (3.7cm) diameter steel tube.
mortar (see estimating table) 1:1:6 mix

Laying out

When you have decided on the position for the barbecue – preferably a flat site – roughly mark out a circle 20' (6m) in diameter and strip off the top soil. Drive a stout stake firmly into the ground as near as possible to the centre of this area. Fix a nail to the stake and attach a 10' (3m) long cord to it. Lay a sand line to mark the circle (see page 92) and then, using the 10' (3m) long cord again, lay out stakes at 10' (3m) centres around the circle (fig. 4).

Use these stakes to mark out the part circles around the circumference. Attach a 6' (1.8m) long cord to each of the stakes and mark a part-circle with sand this distance – this is the inner edge of the seating bays. Repeat again with a length of cord 9'9" (2.8m) to mark the outer circumference of the bays. The space between outer and inner circumferences will be sufficient for planting. The top soil should be stripped also from the remaining areas within the outer curcumference of the seating bays.

Seating: foundations

Dig out the part circles between the sand lines. It should not be necessary for the foundation for these low walls to be excavated to a depth of more than 1' (30cm) below the already stripped ground,

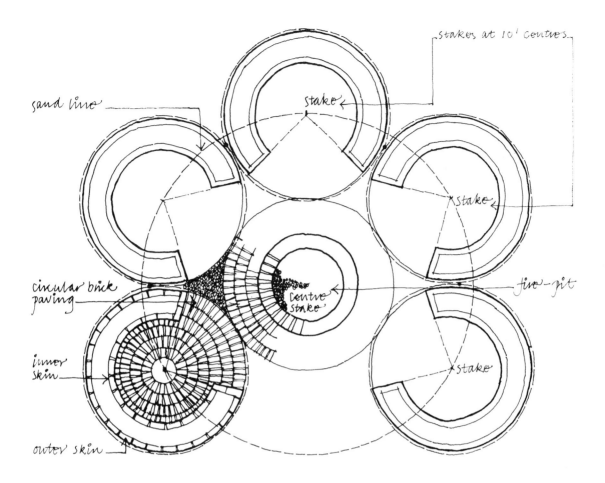

Fig. 4 Laying out plan

provided that the ground is not very soft or loose. If it is, you should dig deeper until it becomes firm and solid. Ram the bottom of each trench with the soil rammer and drive in 1″ × 9″ (2.5cm × 23cm) wooden stakes for levelling. These stakes should project 6″ (15cm) above the trench bottom when the tops are level. Remember, as the foundations are semi-circular, the stakes can only be placed about 3′ (90cm) apart in each trench to allow the straight edge to be placed on them. Check with the spirit level and adjust as necessary.

Next pour the concrete 1:2:4 into the trenches. Level this off to the tops of the stakes. Leave the concrete to set for three or four days.

To make sure the individual foundations for the bays are level with one another, set out level lines horizontally across pairs of bays and measure down from these to the tops of the stakes. Adjust as necessary.

Brickwork

Start with the outside skin of each wall. Spread ½″ (1.2cm) of mortar around the outside of the foundation and, using the centre stake and cord for each semi-circle, make a line in the mortar with a sharpened stick. This will give you a reasonably accurate line along which to lay your bricks. Lay the first course for the outside skin in stretcher (running) bond.

Repeat the marking out process for the inside skin and lay this course stretcher (running) bond as well.

Now lay the first course across at each end, bonding the corners. Continue building up the corners first to a height of approximately 4′ (1m) above foundation level; complete the courses to this height following the curves of the first course. Check frequently with the spirit level and gauge rod.

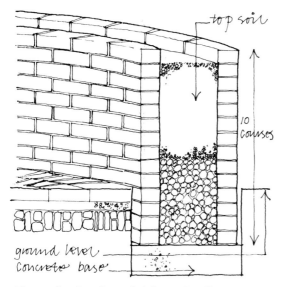

Fig. 5 Section through 'planter' wall

Joint the brickwork as you go, flush jointing first, then finish off slightly recessed. Allow the mortar to harden for about 5 days, then fill the space between the brick skins with stones and rubble to a depth of about 2′ (60cm) which will provide drainage for the planting soil. Then lay 9″ (23cm) of gravel and finish with topsoil mixed with peat.

Fire-pit and base for paving

Drive the tubular steel posts for the flares into the ground where the circles touch.

Dig a hole for the fire-pit in the centre of the area later to be paved. This pit is bowl-shaped measuring 3′6″ (1m) across and 3′ (90cm) deep and will be filled with 1′ (30cm) of rubble and then gravel up to the level of the stripped ground (fig. 6).

Lay 4″ (10cm) of hardcore (or gravel) over the whole area including the spaces in the bays, and

spread 2″ (5cm) of sand over this as a level bed for the brick paving.

The edge of the hardcore (or gravel) around the fire-pit will need to be stiffened to prevent settlement of the brick surround to the fire-pit. To reinforce this edging, mix mortar 1:3 and thoroughly 'plaster' the edge, working the mortar well into the spaces until a ring about 9″ (23cm) wide is bound together with mortar (fig. 8). Bed a course of paving bricks on a $\frac{3}{4}$″ (2cm) mortar bed (instead of sand) around the opening, checking across the pit with the straight edge and spirit level, to ensure it is level.

Fire-pit edging

Build the upstand-edging for the pit as shown in fig. 8. First lay a ring of ordinary bricks flat in a radial formation on individual mortar beds and leave a gap of $1\frac{1}{2}$″ (3.7cm) at the narrowest point between each brick to encourage a flow of air over the surface of the fire. On top, lay a ring of plinth headers flat, with the joints occurring in the centre of the bricks below. Make sure all joints are filled with mortar and strike a flush joint.

Finishing off paving

Lay the circular paving slabs in the centre of each of the bays bedding them on extra sand if necessary to bring the surface up to finished paving level. Working out from these slabs to the fire-pit, lay the circular brick-paving (fig. 7). Bricks will probably have to be cut to fit into the angles at the intersections of the circles. As an alternative method, fill this space with a mortar mix and hand-set 1″ (2.5cm) pebbles touching each other and pressed slightly into the mortar. Then pour a cement grout (cement and sand [1:1] mixed with water to the consistency of thin cream) between the pebbles. Before this has hardened, carefully brush the grout off the pebbles using clean water. Avoid smearing the bricks.

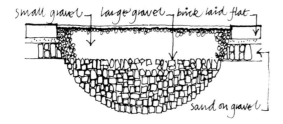

Fig. 6 Section through fire-pit

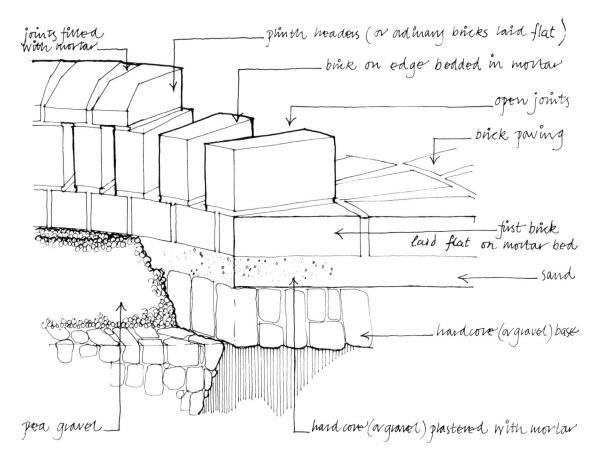

joints filled with mortar

plinth headers (or ordinary bricks laid flat)

brick on edge bedded in mortar

open joints

brick paving

first brick laid flat on mortar bed

sand

hardcore (or gravel) base

pea gravel

hardcore (or gravel) plastered with mortar

Fig. 8   Fire-pit edge detail

**Fig. 7
Brick paving arrangement**

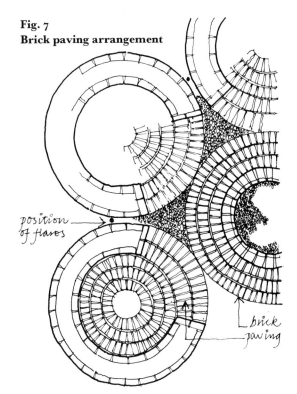

position of flares

brick paving

Screen wall and carport

Open screen walls are ideal for all sorts of situations, from keeping trash cans or installations out of sight, to providing a wind break at the front of your house where a solid wall would be too obtrusive. One of the great advantages of an open screen is that it can provide shelter, while still allowing you to see through it, so this kind of wall is never tiring and never static.

There are many different ways to create screen walls; dozens of decorative screen blocks are made specially for the purpose, but the most adaptable material of all is the ordinary standard brick. So many patterns can result from an arrangement of ordinary bricks; you can lay them either on edge, as in our project, or projecting, or simply leave out bricks in alternate courses. You must make sure that the bonding and strength of the wall will not be too much affected by the arrangements of bricks and space. Of course a long screen wall will need piers (pilasters) just like a solid wall, at strategic points to make it strong.

The open screen effect can be used in other imaginative ways. On page 115 we have illustrated an idea for indoors. This wine-rack and places for storage jars is certainly a novel and simple use of bricks in open arrangements. You can see here how the bricks contribute to the 'country' atmosphere of the dining-area, providing a screen without being too heavy or oppressive, even in this small room.

There are no hard and fast rules for decorative screen walls (besides strength as already mentioned) so it would be fairly easy to design your own according to your own requirements indoors or out. Work out your design on paper first, of course, to make sure it follows through and don't be too ambitious—a simple design is often the most effective.

Getting Started

The brick to be used for an open screen wall must be chosen with care. Remember, you will be seeing both sides of the wall and looking through it as well.

The bricks should be of a similar texture and colour on all faces, without frogs or perforations. The method of firing clay bricks makes this hard to achieve, so buy a brick which comes the nearest to it. Bear in mind the colour of your house and buy a brick similar to this. A smooth or lightly textured wire-cut brick would be suitable; avoid sand-faced bricks where the face is a different colour from the body. This is one case where a visit to a trade showroom would be time well spent.

We have adapted our screen wall to make a carport by adding a concrete floor and corrugated roof. Of course, the screen wall can be built just by itself. You must check with your local building code before you begin, for depths of foundations and widths of footings.

Tools

You will need all the basic tools listed on page 25 plus:
Right-angle square
Short stakes and cord
Gauge rod

Materials

You should use standard-sized solid bricks.
500 common bricks
50 engineering or SW bricks
1500 facing bricks
4 cu yds (3m³) concrete 1:2:4 mix
3 cu yds (2m³) hardcore (or gravel)
Mortar (see estimating table) 1:1:6/1:3 mix
8 galvanized steel joist hangers
154 sq ft (14.3m²) corrugated translucent sheeting.
Screw nails, plastic washers and caps for attaching sheeting
18′ (5.4m) length PVC rainwater gutter, brackets and screws
9′ (2.7m) 3″ (7.5cm) diameter PVC rainwater pipe, fixing clips and screws
40′ (12m) 3″ × 6″ (7.5cm × 15cm) softwood
60′ (18m) 2″ × 5″ (5cm × 12.5cm) softwood

Laying out and foundations

The precise position and length of the wall will obviously depend on the length and width of your car. To allow the car door to be opened, leave 9′ (2.7m) minimum from the screen wall to the side of the existing building.

Lay out batter boards as for a free-standing wall (see page 30) with a building line parallel to the side of the house at a distance of 8′6″ (2.6m). Dig a foundation trench 2′6″ (76cm) deep (or below the frost line) and 1′6″ (45cm) wide.

We will describe how to build an 18′ (5.5m) long half-brick-thick free-standing wall and it will require one stiffening pier (pilaster) at each end

Fig. 1

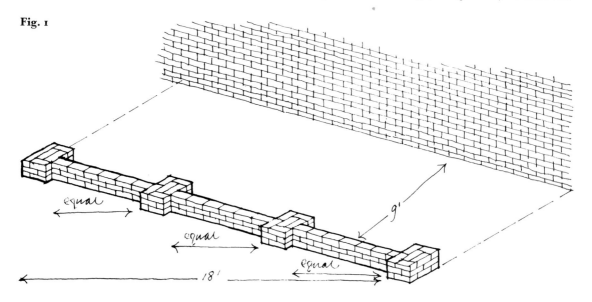

and two in the centre. Where the piers (pilasters) occur the foundation trench must be widened. If you want to build a longer wall consult the 'pier' table on page 36.

Dig out and level the bottom of the trench and lay concrete 1:2:4 6″ (15cm) deep. Allow the concrete to harden for about three days before laying any bricks.

Solid brickwork

Lay the common bricks bedded in mortar 1:3 on the concrete base, bonding in the piers (pilasters) as shown in fig. 3. The wall below ground will be solid and should be bonded in stretcher (running) bond (see page 37). Bed each course in mortar and continue up to an approximate height of 1′9″ (53cm). Now use the facing bricks for two courses and then lay one course of engineering bricks (or SW bricks) as a damp-proof course. The damp-proof course may not be necessary; check your local building code.

If you do not need a damp-proof course continue with the facing bricks but bed this course in mortar 1:1:6.

Floor of carport

If you wish to use your screen wall as a carport, it is now time to prepare the floor. Strip off the topsoil to a depth of about 6″ (15cm) from the space between the new foundation and the house. Backfill the trench around the base of the wall with the previously excavated soil, placing it in 6″ (15cm) layers and ramming it until well compacted.

To form the edge of the slab at each open end, fix temporary forms using 2″ × 6″ (5cm × 15cm) wood nailed to stout stakes driven into the ground about 3′ (90cm) apart. The top edge of the board must finish level with the top of the damp-proof course, or the last course of facing bricks. Check this with the spirit level, and adjust if necessary.

Lay hardcore (or gravel) as a base for the floor slab and ram this well to make sure that there are no large voids. Lay 2″ (5cm) of sand over the hardcore (or gravel) to fill the smaller cavities. This should finish 4″ (10cm) below the level of the last course just laid.

Pour concrete 1:2:4 and spread with the shovel.

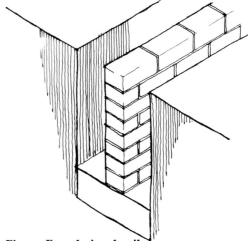

Fig. 2   Foundation detail

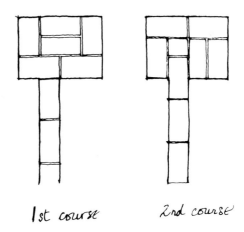

1st course   2nd course

Fig. 3   Alternate courses for end piers

Tamp well with the edge of a board to release any trapped air, consolidate the mix, and achieve a level finish. Refer to pages 62-3 for detailed information on laying the concrete slab. Any hollows or depressions should be filled and re-tamped.

Remember to cover the new concrete with sacking or other material which should be kept damp if the weather is very hot, so that the concrete does not set too rapidly and crack.

Continue now with the brickwork. Lay a course of facing bricks, bedded in mortar 1:1:6. Stagger the vertical joints to maintain the bond and, of course, bond in the piers (pilasters) (figs. 3 and 4). Now build up the end piers for a further three courses and strike a flush joint.

Open brickwork

Now you are ready to lay the first open row of bricks on end. Position these bricks vertically so that the first is bedded directly over a vertical joint in the solid brick course below, the second in the centre of the brick below, the third over the next joint below and so on (fig. 5). Since clean spaces are essential to the open screen effect, a mortar bed cannot be spread on top of the last full course of bricks. Butter the end of each vertical brick separately and carefully place in position making sure it is upright. Lay the next row as a horizontal full course, positioning the vertical joints in the centre of every alternate upright brick. Bond this course with the piers (pilasters) and then build the piers (pilasters) up another three courses. Now lay another row of bricks on end and a full course on top of both vertical bricks and piers (pilasters). Proceed in this manner, checking frequently with the spirit level, until you have reached 7'9" (2.3m) from the concrete slab level. (If you are using a

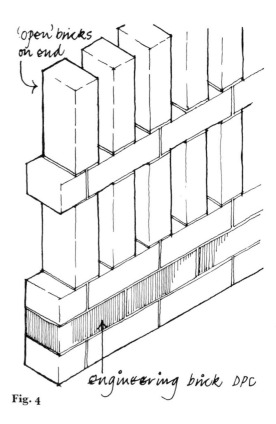

Fig. 4

brick thinner than $2\frac{5}{8}''$ you will have to round up to the next full course.)

Lay one further full course of brickwork along the top of both openwork and piers (pilasters) and finish with a brick-on-end coping course in the normal way (see fig. 6). Since this open wall is obviously not as substantial as a solid wall, it will be comparatively flimsy while being built. We advise you to build half the height and allow four to five days' interval for the mortar to set before continuing with the remainder.

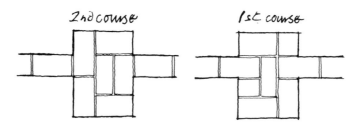

Fig. 5 Alternate courses for intermediate piers

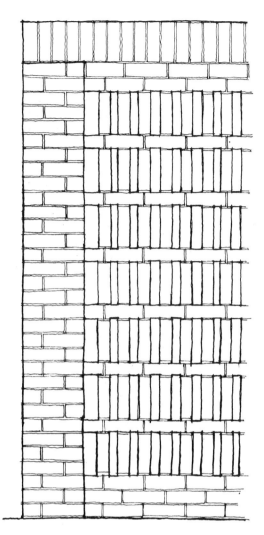

Roof

Complete your carport with a simple roof. Build galvanized steel joist hangers into the brickwork of each pier (pilaster) one brick course down from the top (fig. 8). On the existing wall opposite each pier (pilaster), make a mark on the brick course at, or just above, 8′3″ (2.5m) from the slab. Use a long 2″ × 3″ (5cm × 7.5cm) wooden batten to locate the position precisely.

Carefully chop the brick above each mark with the hammer and brick set (fig. 7). If there is a cavity wall, take great care to prevent pieces of broken brick or large pieces of mortar from

Fig. 7

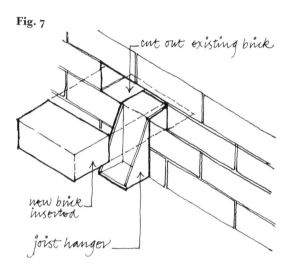

cut out existing brick

new brick inserted

joist hanger

Fig. 6   View of part of wall

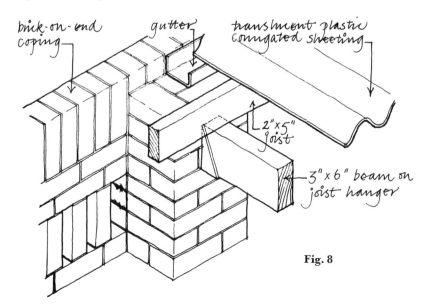

brick-on-end coping

gutter

translucent plastic corrugated sheeting

2″ × 5″ joist

3″ × 6″ beam on joist hanger

Fig. 8

dropping down into it. You may find it easier to remove the brick by cutting out the mortar joints; a number of holes drilled close together will reduce the resistance to the chisel.

Position a joist hanger in each hole. Spread $\frac{3}{4}''$ (2cm) of mortar on the bottom and sides of the holes. Spread mortar also on top of three new bricks and put one in each hole on each joist hanger. Tap into place with the trowel handle. Leave the mortar to harden for three to four days.

Use $3'' \times 6''$ (7.5cm × 15cm) wood for the cross beams and place them in the joist hangers.

Next fix the PVC guttering to the top of the screen wall in the position shown in fig. 8. You will have to decide on the best position for the water outlet, either at one end or the other and attach the rainwater pipe with a 'shoe'. The pipe will take the water from the guttering down into the ground.

Now position wooden joists at right-angles to the main beams. Four equally spaced will be sufficient for a span of 6' (2.4m). These wooden joists should be 2" (5cm) thick and 5" (12.5cm) deep. Attach these to the main beams with 6" (15cm) nails driven at an angle through them (fig. 9). Finally lay translucent, glass-reinforced, corrugated, polyester sheeting on the joists and screw it down through the top of a corrugation, not the valley, using special non-ferrous screws with plastic caps and washers which you will be able to buy from the supplier of the sheeting. (fig. 11). The lower edge of the sheeting should overlap the gutter by about 1" (2.5cm) so that water running down the corrugations can discharge straight into it.

Note: the size of main beams, joists etc. are suitable for the type of roof covering described and dimensions given. If you wish to use a solid roof, or increase the overall dimensions of the carport, then these sizes will have to be increased.

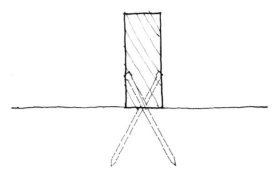

Fig. 9   Joist cross-nailed to beam

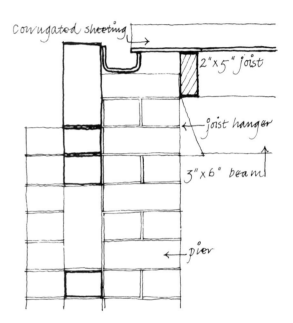

Fig. 10

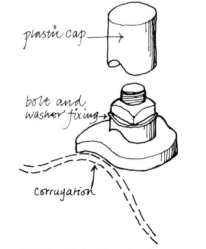

Fig. 11   Detail of fixing for sheeting

The versatile quality of brickwork is evident here: an
open arrangement creates a wine rack and storage places
for jars and at the same time avoids the oppressiveness of
a solid wall in a small area.

Arches

Where an opening like a door or window occurs in brickwork, it is necessary to support the brickwork over it. In the past, the opening was often spanned by a flat beam of wood or stone known as a lintel, or the opening was divided into smaller units with vertical mullions supporting the lintel. Today, a similar method is used but the lintel is made of reinforced concrete or steel, allowing much wider openings. As builders became more aware of the theory of structural forces, the brick or stone arch was widely used, not only to span a simple opening, but also to lighten structures, and avoid massive masonry walls by means of 'relieving arches' to transmit forces at specific positions. The high-point of brick-built arches can be seen in 19th-century railway engineering structures like the viaduct opposite.

Unfortunately, because building arches is a slow and labour-intensive process, it can rarely be justified in cost terms today. The reasons for building arches are purely aesthetic.

Arch-building is really a job for the craftsman; but we can undertake simple arches without too many problems. The width of an opening you intend to span with a brick arch should not exceed 4′ (1.2cm).

We have illustrated some common, simple arch forms on pages 118-9; there are many others but these usually involve much more complicated setting out and construction together with wedge-shaped bricks. We will restrict ourselves to the simpler forms.

For openings wider than 4′ (1.2m), a flat brick arch or 'soldier course', should be used and supported on a steel or concrete lintel with steel angles bolted to it (fig. 2a). This is not a true arch but will maintain the unified appearance of the

View through tunnel of brickwork created by nineteenth-century railway viaduct spanning the Ouse Valley, Sussex, England. The picture is not upside down!

wall. If the opening is wider than 6′ (1.8cm) the brickwork may look as if it is sagging; a very slight upward curve of no more than ½″ (1.2cm) will avoid this optical illusion.

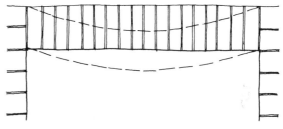

A completely flat arch over a wide opening may appear to sag

Fig. 2b shows a lintel spanning an opening in a cavity wall. Note the cavity gutter which prevents water from reaching the inner skin of the wall.

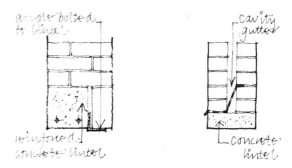

Fig. 2a   Solid wall   **Fig. 2b   Cavity wall**

If the brickwork above an opening is left unsupported, part of the wall above will collapse; the collapsed area will be quite a small triangle of brickwork (fig. 3a). As you can see, the arch does not have a very great load to bear from the brickwork and can be used to carry much greater loads such as floor joists which can be built into the wall just above the opening.

A true arch is built as a number of small units (in

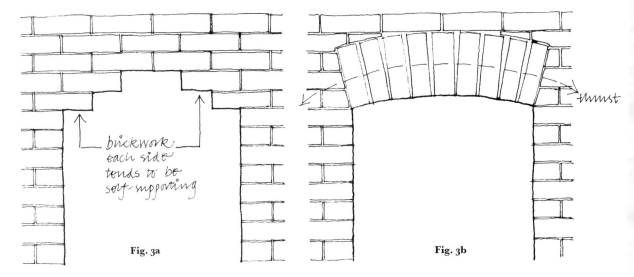

Fig. 3a

Fig. 3b

this case bricks) which press against each other to carry the weight put upon them from above and pass this weight as a thrust to the solid wall on either side (fig. 3b).

To demonstrate this theory, hold five or seven matchboxes between the thumb and second finger, which represent the abutments of the wall, and position a match between each box, right at the top to get the curvature. It's not easy—another hand would help! Now 'load' the top of the matchbox arch, you may be surprised how much pressure is needed to cause a collapse and you will feel the pressure being transmitted through the boxes to your thumb and finger.

There are three principal sorts of arches all of which spring from a single centrepoint on the vertical axis of the opening. An example of each is shown opposite and below.

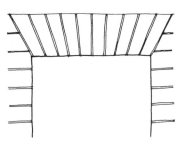

Flat arch. This depends on the use of shaped bricks each side, radiating from the centrepoint. They can either be rubbers or specially-made wedge-shaped bricks.

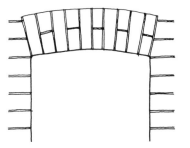

Segmental arch. This is a segment of a much larger (imaginary) circle, again the single radius point is on the vertical axis. The bricks can be wedge-shaped, or the arch can be built of ordinary bricks laid on edge. See page 123.

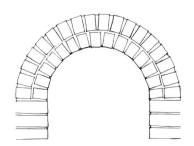

Semi-circular arch. The radius point is on the line of the springing of the arch and in the centre of the opening. The bricks can be normal or specially made.

Except on very high quality or restoration work, the most common way to build arches today is by using normal bricks laid on edge with the mortar joint forming the wedge shape—just like our matchboxes but the space between them is the mortar. This method is known as a rough arch and in earlier, more craft-conscious days, it would only have been used when the wall was going to be plastered over. 'Rough' semi-circular and segmental arches will be the easiest for us to build.

Above left: Flat arch above a window.   *Above right: Two-ringed arch above a window.*

Below: Early 18th-century arcade of semi-circular arches, Powis castle, Wales.

Arch centring

The methods of constructing either a semi-circular or segmental arch are basically the same—both will require temporary supports to be left in place for at least seven days until the mortar has hardened and gained strength.

We will assume an opening 3′6″ (1m) wide to be built in a one-brick-thick solid wall. If you intend to build an arch in a cavity wall you can do it in a similar manner but remember, the arch itself will be solid brick from the outside face through to the inside and would be a likely spot for damp patches appearing on the plaster inside. For this reason we recommend you avoid this.

The temporary forms for the arch are known as centring. They are made of wood and for a semi-circular arch you will need:

1″ × 8″ (2.5cm × 20cm) for ribs—total length 12′6″ (3.5m)
2″ × 4″ (5cm × 10cm) for ties—total length 12′ (3.7m)
1″ × 2″ (2cm × 5cm) for lagging—total length 40′ (12m)
2″ × 3″ (5cm × 7.5cm) for 4 props and 6 bearers
(to work out the total length multiply the height of your opening by four and add on about 8′ (2.4m) for the bearers)
1″ × 3″ (2.5cm × 7.5cm) 9″ (23cm) long for top brace.

For segmental arch (where you can make do with a slightly simpler form of centring):

1″ × 6″ (2.5cm × 15cm) for ribs—total length 8′ (2.4m)
1″ × 2″ (2cm × 5cm) for lagging—total length 20′ (6m)
2″ × 3″ (5cm × 7.5cm) for props and bearers as for semi-circular arch.

Tools

Sabre saw or jig saw
Large pair of compasses. They can be improvized:
    Use a piece of 1″ × 1″ (2.5cm × 2.5cm) wood, drill it to take a crayon and drive a nail into the wood at exactly 1′9″ (53cm) from it.

The centring

You will need two sets of the centring linked together by 1″ × 2″ (2.5cm × 5cm) lagging, as shown in fig. 11. One corresponds to each face of the arch, and so the lagging represents the thickness of the wall; it is by this that the bricks forming the arch will initially be supported.

First make the ribs: take a piece of the 1″ × 8″ (2.5cm × 20cm) wood 6′ (1.8m) long, and half way down cut across it at an angle of 45°. Turn one of the resulting pieces over, fit them together, and they will form the apex of a triangle. Across the triangle nail two pieces of 2″ × 4″ (5cm × 10cm), one across the base of the triangle, and one just below the apex (fig. 7). From the centrepoint of the bottom edge of the bottom tie, mark out a semicircle on the wood with a large pair of compasses, radius 1′9″ (53cm). With the sabre saw or jig saw, cut the semicircle out, sawing where necessary both through the ribs and through the ties—the result should look like fig. 8. Repeat the operation, producing a second semi-circle. In the top or apex of each cut a slot into which you nail the 1″ × 3″ (2.5cm × 7.5cm) centre brace, 9″ (23cm) long, and at the sides at the bottom you join the two semi-circles together with 9″ (23cm) lengths of 2″ × 3″ (5cm × 7.5cm). Finally, cut the 1″ × 2″ (2cm × 5cm) into 9″ (23cm) lengths, and nail these across between the ribs leaving about ½″ (1cm) gap between them.

The procedure for constructing the centring for the segmantal arch is similar but less bracing is required. You will, however, have to set the wooden ribs on a flat floor to mark the curve, the centre of which is some distance away.

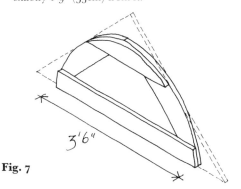

Fig. 7

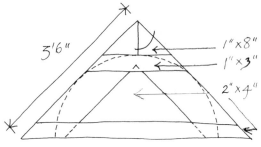

Fig. 8

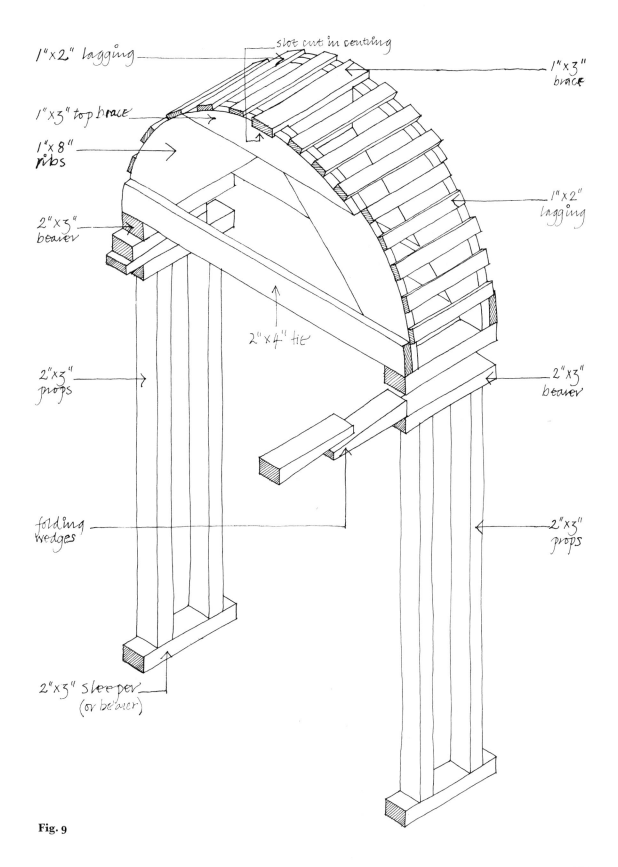

1"x2" lagging

slot cut in centring

1"x3" brace

1"x3" top brace

1"x8" ribs

2"x3" bearer

1"x2" lagging

2"x4" tie

2"x3" props

2"x3" bearer

folding wedges

2"x3" props

2"x3" sleeper (or bearer)

Fig. 9

Building the arch

When you have built up the wall as described on pages 34-5 to ground or floor level, position the sleepers and props. Nail diagonal bracing across, and check with the spirit level to make sure that it is vertical in both directions (fig. 10) as this determines the sides of the brick opening.

Starting from the reveals (sides), build up to the 'springing' of the arch (postion A and B in fig. 10).

Place the arch centring on the bearers using folding wooden wedges (fig. 9). Folding wedges are tapered pieces of $2'' \times 3''$ (5cm × 7.5cm) wood which can be wedged under the centring and knocked out with a mallet when the arch is completed to release the centring from the arch and make dismantling easier.

Brickwork: inner ring

To lay the inner ring of the arch, start at the point of springing. Lay a full brick on its bed against the wooden centring with the narrow face into the arch, place mortar on this first brick and lay the second, tapping with the trowel handle so that the brick tilts with a $\frac{1}{4}''$ (6mm) mortar joint at the narrowest point, and follows the curve of the centring.

Repeat on the other side, building the arch up from the two sides. When you get to the top centre, try and space the bricks so that one whole brick is placed centrally to form the 'keystone'. If there is not room for a whole brick, a few tiles could be used instead, as shown below.

Brickwork: outer ring

Repeat the second ring, spreading mortar from the trowel on the top of the inner ring and bedding the bricks in this, forming wedge-shaped joints between each brick.

The joints between bricks will vary between the two rings. This is inevitable but try to avoid any vertical joints in the two rings coinciding, except either side of the centre brick. Point up as you go. Having completed both rings, continue building up the wall starting from the abutments (fig. 10)

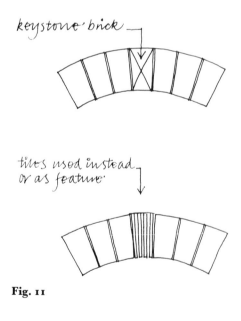

Fig. 11

Fig. 10   The centring in place and the two-ringed arch built

and cutting bricks at a progressively more acute angle to suit the curve. You can build a three-ring arch if you wish. The vertical joints between bricks should follow the general pattern established in the wall as a whole.

Remove the forms after seven days by knocking out the folding wedges and carefully taking out the centring and props.

Finally, rake out the joints to the soffit of the arch and mix a small quantity of mortar and point up using the small pointing trowel to work the mortar into the joint and finishing off in the manner used for the rest of the brickwork.

Follow the same method exactly for the segmental arch.

Three-ringed loadbearing arch.

Pergola

Containing and defining space is a fundamental philosophy of the design of all built environments. It gives us a feeling of 'place' and identity, which we need as much as food and warmth. The cloisters of an abbey are one example of how seclusion and tranquility can be achieved by enclosing space; the atrium or courtyard of a house in ancient Rome, separated from the noisy bustling street only by double gates, is another.

A modern cloister can be created by enclosing the space in the immediate vicinity of your house by a pergola. A pergola is a walkaway built to provide a kind of half-shade—a leafy vault which lets in the sun's rays, yet protects us from strong breezes, a kind of shady perfumed tunnel. Our imagination can easily conjure glorious visions—in summer, roses tumbling from arches, in spring, wistaria hanging in long fragrant ropes, and in autumn, grapes ripening just above our heads; the pergola can be a delight all the year round. Many of the great houses of the 19th century used the pergola to cover a terrace or pathway but in the first half of our own century gardeners rather lost interest in them. Now they are coming back into favour again.

They give an excellent opportunity for imaginative planting—there are so many climbing plants and vines which can be trained up the piers to grow over the canopy. But don't underestimate the need for a really strong top; the weight of flowers and fruit can be considerable. The planting space around each pier should be fertilized and mulched regularly.

Our project can of course be adapted to many individual situations but would best suit a house with a basic 'L'-shaped plan which will form two sides of the courtyard with living rooms opening into it.

The area thus enclosed becomes an extension of the living space, a transition between indoors and garden proper and can be laid out in a different way. For instance, it may be set out as a formal garden with carefully trimmed dwarf hedges, and a fountain perhaps, or it can be paved and used as a secluded patio. Many variations are possible but basically the effect is similar—an additional 'place', not indoors but somehow not quite outdoors either. A super setting for a summer evening party or Sunday morning breakfast.

Getting started

This is a complex project and we recommend that it is attempted only when a reasonable degree of skill with the tools and materials has been achieved. The pergola is formed as a series of arches and niches and so the information on pages 120-22 relating to arch construction will apply here.

Because the lengths of the sides of the 'cloister' will vary, depending on your particular house, we have listed quantities of materials for one bay only, comprising piers and arch with rear niche and based on a 4'6" (1.4m) module. You will have to draw a plan of the 'courtyard' using the 4'6" (1.4m) grid (fig. 1) to see how many bays are needed, and then multiply the quantities by that number.

When you are building, refer constantly to the general arrangement plan on page 133.

Tools

You will need all the basic tools listed on page 25 plus:
Steel tape-measure
Gauge rod
Short stakes and cord
Sabre saw or jig saw
Large pair of compasses

In addition, centring is needed for the arches (see pages 120-21 for how to build it).

You will need about three sets to avoid long delays. (The actual number will depend, of course, on how many arches you wish to build.)

Materials

You should use standard-sized solid bricks.

350 common bricks
2000 facing bricks
75 paving bricks
60 engineering or SW bricks for damp-proof course
½ cu yd (0.35m³) concrete 1:2:4 mix
Mortar (see estimating table) 1:1:6/1:3 mix
⅓ cu yd (0.3m³) pea shingle
7" × 8" (15.5cm × 20cm) wooden bearer 10' (3m) long
Metal ties
Sheet of lead 1'6" (46cm) square
Expanded metal 2 rolls 8" wide
⅔ cu yd (0.6m³) hogging (or gravel)
Rolled steel channel
Steel T section.

Fig. 1 General arrangement plan

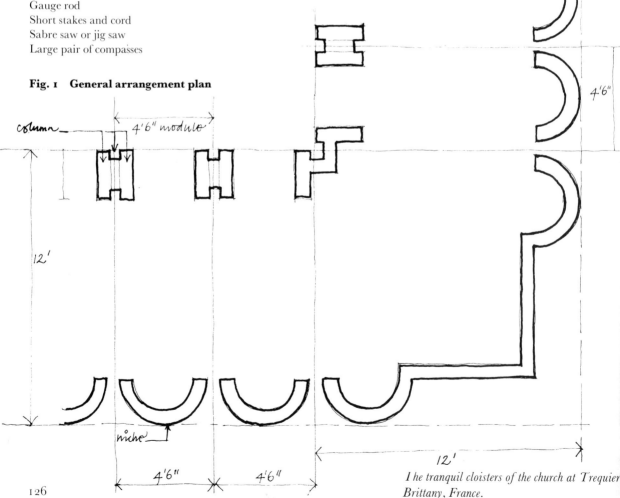

The tranquil cloisters of the church at Trequier Brittany, France.

Laying out and foundations

The first step is to dig the trenches for the columns and niches. To make sure that the brickwork all starts at the same level, the concrete foundation should be a continuous strip rather than individual bases.

Set out lines using the batter board method (page 30). Excavate a trench for the foundations of the columns 2′9″ (84cm) wide and 2′6″ (76cm) deep. Ram and level the bottom.

Now excavate the trench for the semi-circular niches 12′ (3.6m) at the rear of the columns-trench, again 2′9″ (84cm) wide and 2′6″ (76cm) deep.

Drive in 2″ × 2″ (5cm × 5cm) wooden stakes in each trench bottom to project about 6″ (15cm) and level the tops with the spirit level. Mixing concrete by hand will be slow and very hard work because there is so much of it. Use a mechanical mixer or ready-mixed concrete and if possible arrange for it to be poured directly into the trenches. If two or three people are available to help so much the better. Lay the concrete up to the top of the stakes and tamp well. The concrete mix should be 1:2:4. After pouring, leave the concrete for three or four days to set.

Lay out grid lines with cords at right-angles to the building lines across the two trenches at intervals of 4′6″ (1.4m). Each cord will be the centre between adjoining columns and adjoining niches (fig. 1).

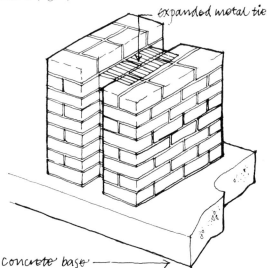

expanded metal tie

concrete base

Fig. 2 Brickwork to column below ground

Brickwork below ground

Column

Each column will consist of two piers, one brick thick by three bricks deep with a half brick in the centre (fig. 2). Each pier will support the side of an adjacent arch.

Lay seven courses of common bricks up to a height of 1′9″ (53.3cm) bedded in mortar 1:3 with expanded metal ties every fourth course. If you are using bricks less than $2\frac{5}{8}″$ in height, lay the number of courses which brings you as near as possible to 1′9″.

Now lay three courses of engineering or SW bricks in mortar for the damp-proof course. Check your local building code; the damp-proof course may not be necessary. If not, continue with the common bricks.

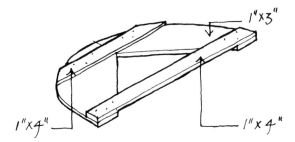

1″×3″

1″×4″

1″ × 4″

Fig. 3 Template for niche

Niche

Construct a wooden template as a semi-circle with a 3′ (90cm) diameter (see page 120). This will help you to achieve the curvature of the niche. Start building the niches, setting the template on the concrete foundation centrally between the grid lines. Lay the common bricks as header courses for the seven courses below ground (fig. 4). With a semi-circle of this radius, the vertical joints on the outer circumference will be about 1″ (2.5cm) wide and may be considered unsightly for facing work. If you wish to avoid this, lay two courses of half-brick rings from the first course below ground level.

After the seventh course lay the damp-proof course, if one is required. Lay three courses of engineering of SW bricks (as half-brick rings). Use the template and make sure the bricks are well bedded in mortar 1:3.

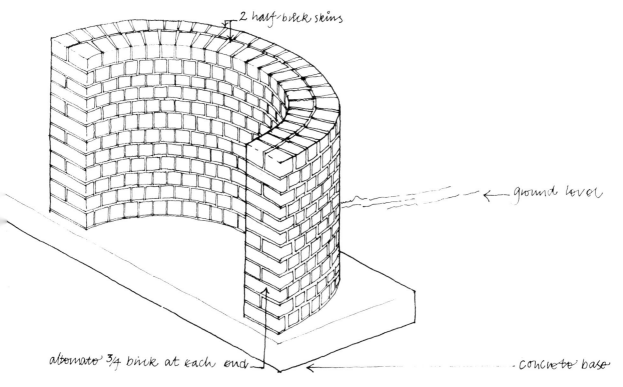

2 half-brick skins

← ground level

alternate ¾ brick at each end

concrete base

Fig. 4   Semi-circular niche

Fig. 5   General arrangement of columns and niches

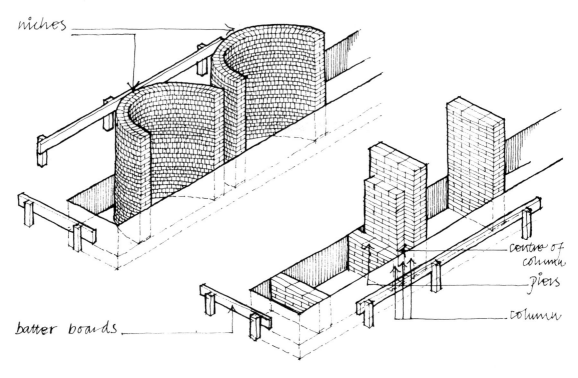

niches

centre of
column
piers

column

batter boards

Brickwork above ground

Back-fill the trenches with the excavated earth, compacting it well with a rammer—the ground may sink later if the fill is loose.

Niche

Continue building up the semi-circular niches with the facing bricks (half-brick rings), bedded in mortar 1:1:6. Use the template to ensure the trueness of the curve and the spirit level to check verticality. Point the brickwork as the work proceeds, with a recessed joint. To ensure that the vertical joints between bricks are staggered, and each joint occurs over the centre of the brick below, begin each alternate course with a three-quarter bat. Where you start with a three-quarter bat you will also finish with one.

Continue building in this manner up to 6′6″ (2m) from ground level or the next nearest course above (fig. 6). Build in short lengths of 6″ × 3″ (15cm × 7.5cm) rolled steel channel painted with black bitumastic paint (fig. 6) and drilled to take a heavy screw. Carry on building six courses from the bedding course of the steel work.

Complete with a course of engineering bricks (or SW bricks) laid on edge for the coping bedded in mortar 1:3.

Columns

Back now to the columns supporting the arches at the front. Continue building these columns using the facing bricks bedded in mortar 1:1:6, bonding the bricks (fig. 2) and setting an expanded metal tie every fourth course. Joint the brickwork with a recessed joint as the work proceeds. Build up to 6′6″ (2m) (or the next nearest course above) from ground level.

Construct the centring for the arches 2′3″ (68.6cm) deep to support the full depth of the arch and 3′ (90cm) wide (fig. 7).

Follow the earlier explanation on page 121 for supporting the centring with props, stretchers and folding wedges. Since the centring must be left in position for one week after the brickwork is completed, it will speed construction to make three sets which can be used in rotation.

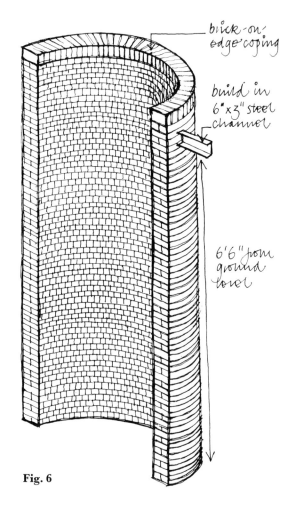

Fig. 6

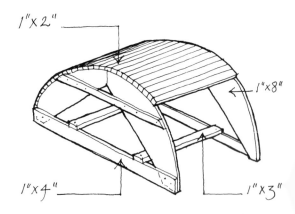

Fig. 7 Arch centring

Arch

It should be possible to plan the construction work so that you can build two columns and an arch followed by a niche and then to the next column and arch.

At this 6'6" (2m) level, which will be four courses below the springing of the arch, place an expanded lead tray on top of the two piers of each column. This will protect the exposed top of the centre of the column from the large quantities of water which will run down the arches and collect on the brickwork. To make the tray, shape a sheet of lead 1'6" (46cm) square into a tray with a hammer and piece of wood. Lead is quite soft and malleable and this should be easy to do. Leave out the centre brick between the two piers for this course and rest the tray on the brickwork (fig. 8).

At this level build in a short length of steel 'T' section drilled to take a heavy screw and painted with black bitumastic paint (fig. 8). The 'T' section can measure either 3" × 3" (7.5cm × 7.5cm) or 2½" × 2½" (6.3cm × 6.3cm) whichever is nearer the size of one of your bricks. The 'T' section should fit into the brickwork in place of one brick without disturbing the arrangement of courses above and below.

Construct the arches as described in detail on pages 122-3. Lay the courses as bricks on edge. The first course will be two full bricks and followed by a half brick. The second course will be a half brick followed by two full bricks, then a half brick. Continue in this manner until the inner arch is complete. Then lay an expanded metal sheet 2' (60cm) wide over the whole inner arch as reinforcement and complete the outer ring, like the inner ring but with the sequence reversed (fig. 10).

Flush joint the top face of the arch. The top of the arch will be very exposed to the weather and will frequently become saturated. This is why the top should be as smooth as possible with flush joints so that water can run off quickly, and not be trapped in the brickwork where it might freeze and cause damage by expansion. For protection, without affecting appearance, the upper surface of the arches should be treated with two coats of a clear silicone liquid.

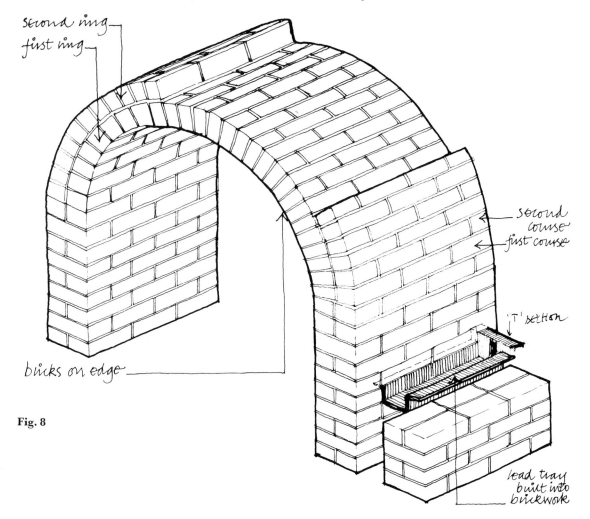

second ring

first ring

second course

first course

'T' section

bricks on edge

lead tray built into brickwork

Fig. 8

Floor

It now remains to complete the floor and the roofing to provide shade.

If you wish, you can lay a brick paving between the arches bedded in mortar 1:3 on a 4″ (10cm) concrete base. Refer to pages 56-77 for ideas and how-to's on pavings. A pocket for climbing plants can be formed on the inside of each double column with a simple brick edging (fig. 10).

Similarly the semi-circle formed by the niches can also be used for planting. The ground for planting will, of course, require good quality topsoil.

Any good gardening book will help you identify suitable climbing plants for your particular climatic conditions.

Lay 4″ (10cm) of hogging (or gravel) spread evenly over the area of the path after you have removed the topsoil, and roll well with a medium roller. Now lay pea gravel for a depth of 3′ (7.5cm). Rake until level and roll lightly.

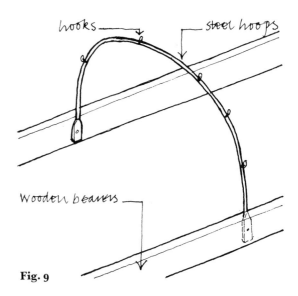

Fig. 9

Fig 10 Detail of the edging

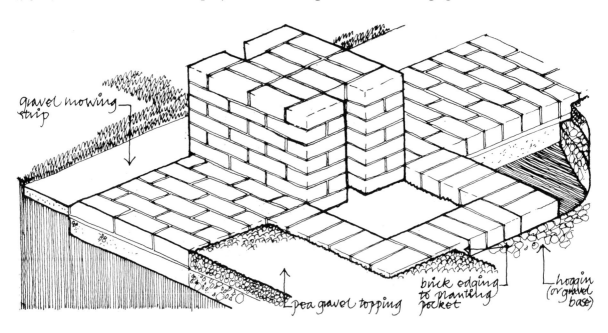

Roofing

Coat the wooden bearers with a preservative or preservative stain. Check with the manufacturer that the preservative will not be harmful to plants. Do not use creosote which, although very good for preventing decay in the wood, will 'burn' the plant foliage.

Position the bearers on the steel supports already built into the brickwork and screw up into them from the holes in the steelwork with large 3″ (7.5cm) sheradized screws.

There are many alternatives for providing training wires and lattices to give some shading to the walk and support climbing plants, but we propose the following:

Use ¼″ (6mm) diameter steel rods 12′ (3.7m) long with each end flattened. To flatten the ends, heat until red-hot with a blow lamp, or brazier, and hammer them flat on a make-shift anvil with a heavy hammer and drill a hole in each end. Measure off at 1′ (30cm) intervals along the rods

and weld a small hook-eye at each point (fig. 9). If you do not have access to, or experience with welding equipment, then take the rods to a local ironworker who will do this for a nominal charge.

At this point the rods should ideally be hot dip galvanized. Look in Yellow Pages for addresses of people who can do this, but if you have no luck, paint the rods with either cold galvanizing paint or black bitumastic.

Allow five rods per bay and screw one end firmly to the inside face of a beam. Gently bend the other end to 'spring' it between the beams and screw this end to the opposite beam. When all the hoops have been formed, attach a galvanized wire to one hook and pass it through the others, securing the other end at the last eye. When this has been completed you will have a very good base to support climbing plants and when the planting is established you will have a beautiful cool and shady walk under leafy vaults.

Fig. 11   View of pergola

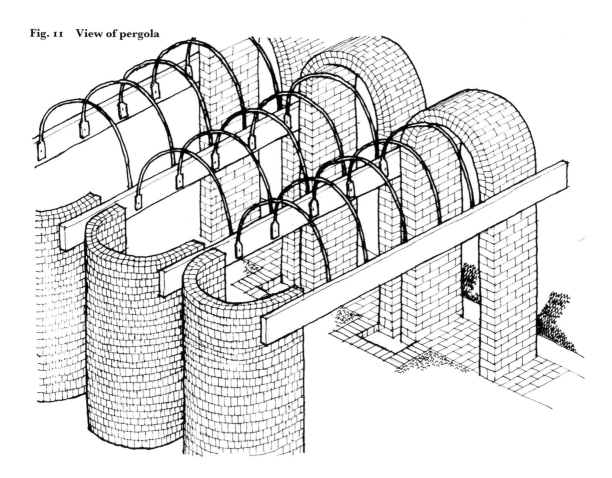

Summer house

The summer house, gazebo, kiosk, whatever name you care to give it has been a feature of many a fine garden for hundreds of years. From the day when the early European Renaissance landscape architect arranged his gardens in strong geometrical designs up to the present day, it has been a place for shade, relaxation and a vantage point from which to view the magnificence of the garden landscape. In 16th-century America, when large parts of the country were still untamed, the great gardens were enclosed by walls to keep out intruders and wild animals and the gazebo was situated in a corner of one of the walls so that women and children could gaze out onto the wilderness beyond. Today it provides an area where you can sit in peace, write letters, or just absorb inspiration from the glorious vegetation growing everywhere in your garden, and contemplate the hard work that has gone into it. It is a congenial place to entertain friends on hot summer days or, on warm summer evenings, to sit and watch the sun go down.

Summer houses have been made from every conceivable material: wood, stone, brick, wrought iron and lattice work, and in every conceivable shape: square, hexagonal, octagonal. We have chosen octagonal, the shape which fired the imagination of architects in America in the 19th century for their domestic building, especially a man of enormous originality Orson Squire Fowler who, in 1849, wrote a treatise called 'A House for all, or the gravel wall and octagon mode of building'. He argued that eight walls enclosed more space than four, inscribed in the same circumference; a house this shape received more daylight, was easier to heat, cooler in summer, being ventilated through a central cupola and was safer in high winds. Many eight-sided houses were built in America in the 1850s and were without exception the choice of the individualist.

Pay particular attention to the siting of your

summer house. We recommend that it should not be nearer than 40′ (12m) from the house. Consider whether you wish it to occupy a symmetrical position with regard to your garden or whether an asymmetrical arrangement might be better.

If you decide on the first approach, choose an important axis relating to the house, i.e. a drive or terrace and centre the summer house on this. If you feel an asymmetrical position is best you can make use of natural features, like a rise or hollow in the ground, the summer house being glimpsed

through a clump of trees. Whichever approach you choose, a backdrop of trees or shrubbery will make the structure blend in a natural way with the ground.

Our design does not provide a completely weatherproof structure but you could adapt it fairly easily. To keep out insects erect mesh screens. Furnish it with chairs, and tables made of bamboo or copies of 19th-century cast-iron and introduce lots of plants in tubs, and hanging baskets; in the evening soft candlelight or garden lights will help to create a congenial atmosphere. Perhaps folding screens will add a feeling of protection when darkness falls.

We have designed the roof so that bamboo matting can be fixed to the roof beams; the further from the centre, the more the bamboo will sag, but this will enhance, rather than detract from, its appeal. For the floor we have suggested ceramic floor tiles but anything attractive and hardwearing can be used.

Getting started

We use brick and wood as the basic materials for our summer house and we recommend ceramic mosaic tiles for the flooring. It is a simple beam and column structure; a building principle still more commonly used in modern architecture than any other.

Wherever you live you will have to carry out certain essential procedures before you start to build. In the U.S. you must check local building codes for depth of foundations and width of footings etc. You must also check with the local building authority about the particular planning legislation requirements in your area. You may find that a permit is not required for an unenclosed structure such as this, but make sure. In the U.K. consent under the Town and Country Planning Act will be necessary whether the structure is enclosed or not. You will have to submit drawings to the Planning Officer showing the siting of the summer house, explaining the scheme and indicating the type and colour of materials to be used. A planning form will also have to be completed.

Before you start digging, make sure that there are no main services: gas, electricity etc. or drainage across the chosen site. If your home is newly built, the original drawings should show the position of all these. If it is an old one, it will be more difficult to find out. As a general rule, gas, electricity and water supply will be at the front of the property, i.e. leading from the street. Drainage may be partly at the back of the house especially if the kitchen or bathroom are at the back; the route of these drains can sometimes be checked by the line of the manhole covers. One common method of draining rainwater is by means of drywells or soakaways which are deep pits filled with rubble into which pipes discharge rainwater from roofs, paths etc. They should be at least 15′ (4.5m) from the house and, as we do not recommend that you build your summer house less than 40′ (12m) away from the house, there should be little chance of encountering a drywell drain.

Choose facing bricks to tone with the rest of the brickwork in your garden and house. They should be a regular shape and size to make the construction of the slender columns simpler. Machine-made bricks are ideal but if you prefer any other kind of brick then it should be 'first hard' which means that it is regular in shape and size. If you

wish to use the same brick for both columns and steps, then a fairly had-burnt brick is necessary and it must not be a sand-faced facing. Mortar joints should only be slightly recessed, not more than $\frac{1}{4}''$ (6mm) just sufficient to emphasize the texture of the brickwork.

Use clear, selected redwood. Apply one coat of preservative or stain before positioning the beams and two after.

Tools

You will need all the basic tools listed on page 25 plus:
Steel tape-measure
Short stakes and cord
Tamping board
Bat-and-closer gauge
Gauge rod

Materials

You should use standard-sized solid bricks.
1000 common bricks
3000 facing bricks (for columns and steps)
2000 single cant facings (or ordinary bricks)
250 engineering or SW bricks

Wood

2″ × 8″ (5cm × 20cm)	8 12′ (3.6m) lengths
1½″ × 4″ (3.7cm × 10cm)	16 12′ (3.6m) lengths
2″ × 3″ (5cm × 7.5cm)	8 2′6″ (75cm) lengths
2″ × 2″ (5cm × 5cm)	16 2′ (60cm) lengths
3″ × 6″ (7.5cm × 15cm)	8 2′ (60cm) lengths

5 galls (23 lit) preservative or stain
22 cu yds (17m³) hardcore (or gravel)
27 cu yds (20m³) concrete 1:2:4 mix
mortar (see estimating table) 1:1:6/1:3 mix
16 1½″ × 6″ (3.7cm × 15cm) galvanized joist hangers

compression ring—(purpose made) from 1½″ × 3″ (3.7cm × 7.5cm) steel angle
54 expanded metal ties—cut from an 8″ (20cm) wide metal roll
8 angle cleats—2″ (5cm) cleats cut from 2″ × 2″ (5cm × 5cm) angle
16 bolts—$\frac{3}{8}''$ (1cm) diameter, 5″ (12.5cm)
ceramic floor tiles.

Laying out and foundations

Roughly mark out the area of the summer house as a circle and excavate the top 6″ (15cm) of soil. Although the floor level will be raised above the surrounding garden this is still necessary to prevent weeds growing, and also because topsoil is soft and easily compressible and may cause cracking in the slab.

Drive a stout stake with a 4″ (10cm) nail in the top firmly into the ground approximately in the centre of the cleared area. Attach a cord to the nail and measure off a length of 9′9″ (3m) along it and drive another stake with a nail in the top at least 3′ (90cm) into the ground at this point. This will be the centre of the first column. To give you the position of the second column, attach a cord exactly 17′2″ (5.25m) long to the nails in the two stakes, with one end attached to each nail; mark the cord at a distance of 9′9″ (3m) from the centre stake; wind the cord round another stake and nail exactly at this point and pull up the slack to form a triangle. When the cord is taut, drive this third stake into the ground. You will now have an isosceles triangle with two sides (from centre stake) of 9′9″ (3m) and a base of 7′5½″ (2.27m) giving the centrepoints of the first two columns.

Check with the tape measure. Repeat until there are eight stakes firmly driven into the ground. Check each one and sight them across the centre stake, making sure that the three stakes are dead in line; level across the tops using a spirit level and a long straight edge.

Excavate a hole 2′6″ (72cm) square and 2′ deep (60cm) around each stake. Measure down from the top of the stakes and make a mark equal on each about 9″ from the bottom of the excavation: this will be the top of the concrete. Lay concrete in each base and level off the top surface at the mark on the stake. Check the dimensions of the stakes again to make sure they have not moved during excavation or pouring the concrete. Leave the concrete for three to four days before starting the brickwork.

Fig. 1   General arrangement plan

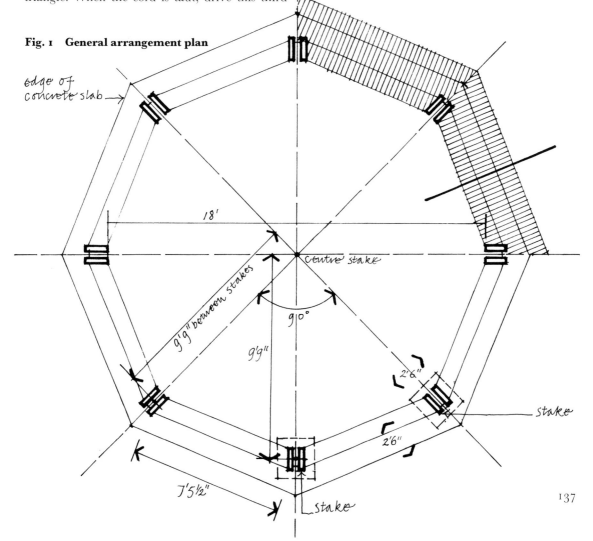

edge of concrete slab →

18′

9′9″ between stakes

centre stake

9′9″

90°

2′6″

2′6″

stake

7′5½″

stake

Column bases

Now lay out the brickwork for the columns accurately. The stakes with nails should still be in position in the concrete. Attach cords to each nail and connect to the one diametrically opposite. They should cross exactly on the centre stake. Each stake will be at the centre of a brick column. The brick columns are $2\frac{1}{2}$ bricks by $1\frac{1}{2}$ bricks with a full brick in the centre (fig. 4). Mark these dimensions out on the concrete base with a heavy wax crayon and chop off the stakes protruding from the concrete.

Using common bricks lay the first course bedding the bricks on the concrete base with mortar 1:3. All joints should be $\frac{3}{8}''$ (1cm) thick. Build up the brickwork, checking with the gauge rod that it rises the correct number of courses for a given height. Lay an expanded metal $8'' \times 12''$ (20cm × 30.5cm) across the brickwork every fourth course. Continue up to $3'3''$ (or the nearest course to this height) which will bring the columns up to floor slab level.

Slab edge and steps

The first step is to construct the wooden forms against which the concrete for the steps will be cast. The quality of wood is not important but it must be strong enough not to collapse under the pressure of the wet concrete. The boards should be $6'' \times 1\frac{1}{2}''$ (15cm × 3cm) and the stakes not less than $2'' \times 2''$ (5cm × 5cm) in three lengths: $2'6''$, $2'$ and $1'6''$ (76cm, 60cm, and 46cm). Starting on the top row, drive the longest stakes about $1'$ (30cm) into the ground, $3'$ (90cm) apart with a stake occurring at each end of a board, and forming the angles of the octagon (fig. 3). Nail the boards to the stakes and use the spirit level to ensure that the tops of the boards are level. Repeat for the next two steps: the top edge of the lower board in each case should be in line with the lower edge of the board above.

Place hardcore (or gravel) over the whole area of the floor to a thickness of $1'6''$ (46cm) roughly sloping off the edges under the steps. The hardcore (or gravel) should be faced with $2''$ (5cm) of sand. Now cast the concrete slab and steps; the concrete for the steps should not be less than $6''$ at its shallower point. Allow four to five days before removing the forms.

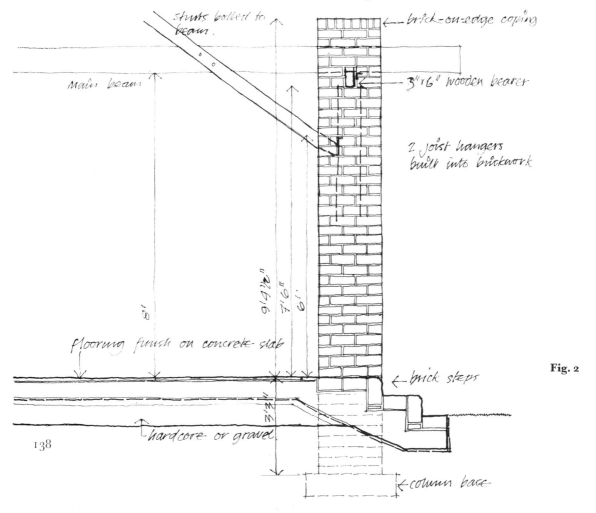

Fig. 2

Brickwork for columns

Build up the columns with facing bricks bedding them in mortar 1:1:6. On each column lay two courses following the same pattern as that for the brickwork up to slab level and then lay a damp-proof layer if required. This should be heavy black PVC or a bituminous inorganic felt. Continue building up the columns, checking verticality and gauge as before. Every foot (30cm) lay $8'' \times 12''$ (20cm × 30cm) expanded metal reinforcement ties across the columns as shown in fig. 4. As a column reaches about half full height move on to the next. Build in a joist hanger at the height indicated in fig. 2 and the $6'' \times 3''$ (15cm × 7.5cm) wooden bearers to support the main beams at $7'6''$ (2.2m) from the slab.

Continue building up the two outside brick skins (wythes) for four courses, omitting the centre brick. For the coping cut half bricks from the engineering or SW bricks and bed on the cut end. Joints between bricks will have to be increased to cover the $1'10\frac{1}{2}''$ (57.2cm) depth across the top of the column.

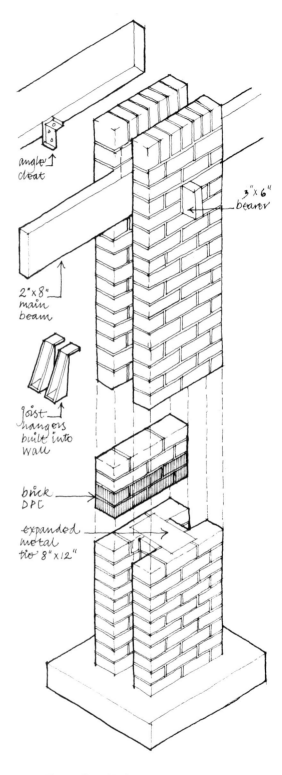

angle cleat

$3'' \times 6''$ bearer

$2'' \times 8''$ main beam

joist hangers built into wall

brick DPC

expanded metal tie $8'' \times 12''$

Fig. 4   Detail of column

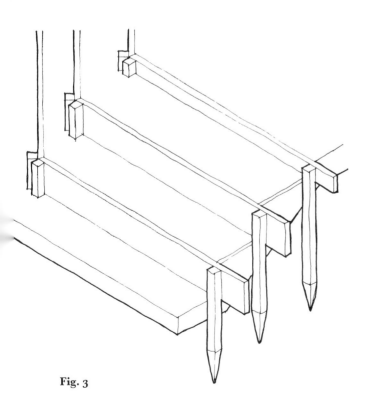

Fig. 3

Roof

Select eight lengths of the $2'' \times 8''$ (5cm × 20cm) wood for the main horizontal beams and cut these to 13′6″ (4.1m). Apply one coat of clear preservative or, if the wood is to be stained, one coat of the preservative stain. Four of the beams should have the edges mitre cut at 45° to fit into the intersection of the other beams at the centre.

Locate the positions for the angle cleats (fig. 4) and screw them to the underside of each beam. Note that a small variation of about 1″ (2.5cm) will occur as a result of the intersection of the beams.

The cleats should be located at 9′10½″ (3.12m) on two beams and 9′9½″ (3.04m) on six. Construct temporary support for the intersection of these beams from long pieces of wood stretching up from slab level. Position the beams on this and the short bearers within the columns. The temporary supports will remain until the roof structure is complete.

Cut the lengths of $1\frac{1}{2}'' \times 4''$ (3.7cm × 10cm) wood for the struts 11′ (3.3m) long and cut the ends at an angle of 50° to the length; notch the ends to fit over the pre-fabricated steel compression ring. Position one strut each side of a main beam with the base supported in the joist hangers. Temporarily support these sloping struts and screw the compression ring in the notched ends. Drill through the struts and beam and insert $2\frac{3}{8}''$ (1cm) diameter bolts.

From a point 6″ (15cm) down each pair of struts position a piece of $2'' \times 2''$ (5cm × 5cm) wood 2′ (60cm) long, as a hanger. Drill through and bolt each time. From this hanger, bolt two pieces of $2'' \times 3''$ (5cm × 7.5cm) wood 2′6″ (75cm) long to drop either side of the $2'' \times 3''$ (5cm × 7.5cm) main beams to which they must again be bolted. Cross spike the intersection of main beams with 6″ (15cm) nails driven at an angle through adjoining beams. The temporary supports can now be removed and the whole roof structure given a final coat of colourless preservative or stain.

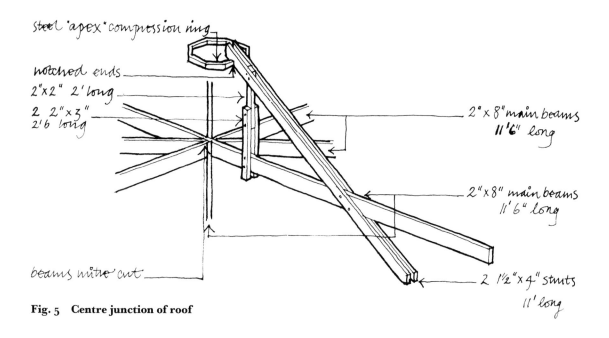

Fig. 5 Centre junction of roof

Steps and floor

The brickwork to the steps and the flooring are the final operations in the project. Read the sections on paving (pages 58-77) and steps (pages 52-5) before you begin.

Start from the top step. Mark the centre of the length of the step and work outwards to each corner. Bed the bricks on edge in mortar 1:1:6. Lift a full trowel of mortar and lay this on the concrete step; next 'butter' the brick on one side with mortar and place down on the mortar bed, tapping into place with the trowel handle. Continue to each end where you will have to cut the bricks to an angle of 60° to achieve the mitred joint. The top step will be two bricks wide. Use the spirit level to achieve a flat surface.

Form the riser to the step by using single-cant bricks on end. If these are not available, or prohibitively expensive, use ordinary facing bricks. It will be necessary to provide packing under the brick to bring the top level with the flat

step. This can be brick tile slips or tiles about 1″ (2.5cm) thick. When laying, make sure that the joints line through. Repeat, working in sequence from the top to the base. Flush joint as the work proceeds and clean off surplus mortar from the brick face.

The top step will be $1\frac{1}{2}''$ (3.7cm) above the concrete slab. Coat the surface of the slab with cement grout, i.e. cement and water mixed to the consistency of thin cream. Lay the frost-proof tiles on a mortar bed; they will have to be mitre cut along the radial lines of the octagon. The depth of your mortar bed will depend on the thickness of the floor finish you intend to use; adjustments will have to be made. If we assume here that your tiles are $\frac{5}{8}''$ (1.6cm) thick, then, to make up the $1\frac{1}{2}''$ (3.7cm) upstand from the concrete slab to the top step, your mortar bed will be $\frac{7}{8}''$ (2.2cm) thick.

Floor laying is a specialist trade and achieving a level, flat surface is not easy; seek specialist advice if you encounter any problems.

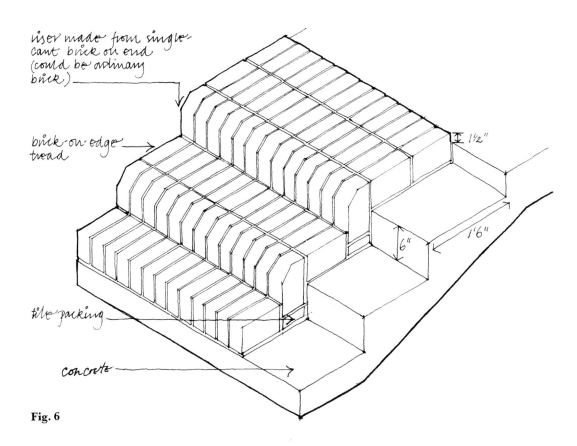

riser made from single-cant brick on end (could be ordinary brick)

brick-on-edge tread

tile packing

concrete

$1\frac{1}{2}''$

6″

1′6″

Fig. 6

Garden room

Today a garden room is whatever you choose to make it—a semi-conservatory for growing pot plants and propogating seeds, a family room with tables for games and drinks, cane chairs to doze in and swing sofas to read in, an almost-terrace set with lacy metal chairs on a white tile floor, and filled with hanging and standing plants of every kind, an extra entertaining space to have a drink before dinner or coffee afterwards, with low floor lamps and lights set in the garden outside.

So first of all, decide what you and your family need most, remembering that, however you use it, the basic contents should be as simple, as versatile and as welcoming as possible. And here once more the magnificent quality or brickwork becomes most evident.

Our garden room has a light, airy Mediterranean feeling and your choice of brick colour would certainly add to this. A pale pinkish or sand-faced brick with toning mortar might be a good choice. Any choice of facing brick will be successful so long as you keep in mind the surrounding walls, but the bricks must have a high frost resistance and low water absorption. After the floor screed has been laid, we suggest for comfort that you carpet the interior.

Getting started

We have designed our garden room as a pavilion, an extra entertaining area, adjacent to a pool for instance, but it could be built as an extension to a house. It is not possible to suggest how to do this here since obviously too many assumptions about a particular house would have to be made and may be disastrously misleading.

It is designed 'in the grand manner' and should be set in a spacious site or against a large house which will not be over-powered by it. It is a complex project and should not be undertaken by anyone who has not had considerable experience with this kind of construction work.

This garden room will certainly require a building permit in the U.S. or, in the U.K., planning consent and building regulation approval. It is important that you get these approvals before starting work. Many instances of worry and disappointment can be cited where enthusiasm to get going, and a contempt for bureaucracy, have brought the wrath of the building department upon the unfortunate constructor!

You will have to submit drawings explaining the method and details of construction, the materials to be used and the colours. In addition there are forms to be completed which can be obtained from the relevant authority who will give you considerable advice and assistance.

Ideally you should ask your architect to submit a scheme but do not tell him to draw up the plans. You will be paying his fee for his talent in interpreting your requirements, but emphasize to the building authority that you will be doing the work yourself.

It is important also to check your local building code for depth of foundations, width of footings and other requirements related to your frost line. If you live in an area that habitually has higher than average wind speeds, or if you live on a very exposed site, you must get a structural engineer to check that the 'holding down' provisions for the roof are adequate.

Your garden room could be left as an open structure, if you live in a particularly warm climate; if not you should have it glazed by specialist glaziers who will probably do it on a 'supply and fix' basis. You will also need electrical installation for lighting and some form of heating. None of these can be dealt with in detail here and you must seek specialist advice.

Tools

You will need all the basic and special tools listed on page 25. There is a lot of wood to cut and power tools would be essential for this and for drilling holes in both wood and masonry.

Materials

Figs. 1-3 show details of special items listed under materials which will have to be purpose-made. Take the drawings along to a local specialist for making up.
You should use standard-sized solid bricks
1350 common bricks
600 facing bricks
1200 bullnose bricks (or ordinary bricks)
6300 paving bricks
30′ (9m) 4″ (10cm) diameter PVC drainage pipe
8 rolls expanded metal strip 8″ (20cm) wide
27 cu yds (20m³) concrete 1:1:4 mix
32 cu yds (24m³) hardcore (or gravel)
8 metal shoes (see fig. 3b)
8 metal holding-down ties (see fig. 3c)
2 11′ (3.3m) 4″ (10cm) diameter aluminium rainwater pipes
200 yds (61m) glass fibre insulation 2′ (60cm) wide
mortar (see estimating table) and coloured mortar for pointing 1:1:6/1:3 mix
16 $\frac{3}{8}$″ × 3″ (1cm × 7.5cm) rawlbolts
24 $\frac{1}{2}$″ × 2$\frac{1}{2}$″ (1.2cm × 7.3cm) rawlbolts (see fig. 3a)
180′ (164.5m) pre-formed aluminium edge trim (see fig. 1)

Wood
700′ (214m) 2″ × 6″ (5cm × 15cm) softwood for joists 15′ (4.5m) long (46 of them)
570′ (174m) 2″ × 6″ (5cm × 15cm) softwood for joists 17′ (5.1m) long (46 of them)
55 8′ × 4′ (2.4m × 1.2m) sheets $\frac{1}{2}$″ (1.2cm) plywood for roof decking
600′ (180m) 2′ × 3″ (5cm × 7.5cm) softwood for firrings
192 $\frac{3}{4}$″ (2cm) plywood gussets
168′ (51m) 2″ × 4″ (5cm × 10cm) chamfered softwood for upstand
168′ (51m) 1″ × 2″ 2.5cm × 5cm) softwood for runners
8 sheets 4′ × 10′ (1.2m × 3m) $\frac{1}{2}$″ (1.2cm) marine plywood for fascia
11,000′ (3,351m) $\frac{3}{4}$″ × 2″ (2cm × 5cm) wooden strip for soffit

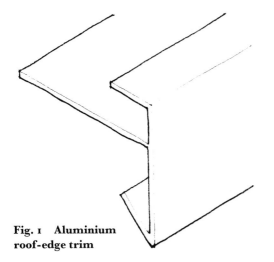

Fig. 1 Aluminium roof-edge trim

Plywood box beams

The main roof beams will be constructed as box beams amd must be made by a specialist. The total length of a beam is 38′ (11.5m). Wood is not available in such lengths, so three lengths will have to be joined together to achieve this. It is most important that the joints occur at the position of least stress.

Four of these beams are required and they will be very heavy. You will need lifting tackle to put them in place and help from three or four friends.

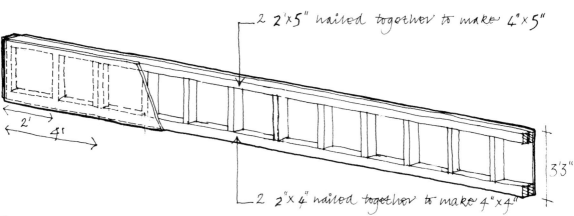

2 2′×5″ nailed together to make 4″×5″

2 2″×4″ nailed together to make 4″×4″

2′ 4′ 3′3″

Fig. 2

Bolts

16 $\frac{3}{8}''\times 3''$. (1cm × 7.5cm) rawlbolts are needed for bolting down the shoes to the columns, and 24 $\frac{1}{2}''\times 2\frac{1}{2}''$ (1.2cm × 7.5cm) rawlbolts are needed for bolting the ties to the brick columns. These are in two parts: the bolt itself; and the socket which is made from cast steel. The socket is inserted into the hole which has been drilled for it and, as the bolt is tightened, the socket expands, firmly gripping the sides of the hole (fig. 3a).

Fig. 3a

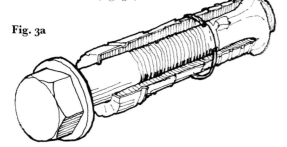

Shoes

Eight welded steel shoes (fig. 3b) are needed to hold the main roof beams on the columns. They will have to be purpose made by a local metal-worker and should preferably be hot dip galvanized after welding. Or they can be painted with a cold 'galvanizing' paint and black bitumastic before you bolt them down on the columns.

Fig. 3b

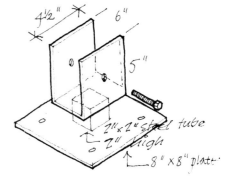

4½″ 6″ 5″ *2″×2″ steel tube 2″ high* *8″×8″ plate*

Holding down ties

Sixteen curved steel ties (fig. 3c) one also needed to prevent very high winds from lifting the roof. They will have to be purpose-made and should be drilled to take rawlbolts and coach screws before galvanizing.

Laying out and levelling

When you have decided on the position for the garden room, roughly mark out a square 45′ × 45′ (14.75cm × 14.75cm) and strip the top soil to a depth of 6′ (15cm). Maybe you can use this topsoil for landscaping elsewhere; if not arrange for it to be taken away. There is always a demand for good topsoil. The excavated area should be approximately level. Check by driving in stakes and using a 1″ × 6″ (2.5cm × 15cm) board with a planed edge and about 10′ (3m) long as a straight edge. Place this on the top of the stakes and put the spirit level on the board; adjust the stakes as necessary until the spirit level reads horizontal. Repeat this across the excavated site until you are satisfied that the ground is reasonably level.

The layout for the column bases is done with batter boards, so read pages 29-30 before you begin. Lay out a cord with short stakes at each end—a building line AB. The distance between the stakes should be 33′ (10m). Use the right-angle square to construct a second building line BC 38′ (11.6m). The diagonal distance between A and C

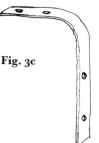

Fig. 3c

¼″ × 2″ galvanised ties drilled to bolt to brick column and coach screw to underside of beam.

should be 50′4″ (15.31m). Now using the square set out point D using the same method. Check that the dimensions between C and D is also 33′ (10m) and the diagonal between B and D is 50′4″ (15.31m). 4′ (1m) outside each of the corner stakes ABCD erect a batter board. Make them from two 1″ × 6″ (2.5cm × 15cm) boards each 7′ (2m) long.

Check that they are level using a long straight edge and spirit level. The distance between the batter boards will be too great for a straight edge and so intermediate wooden stakes should be driven into the ground between the batter boards and adjusted as necessary to obtain a level.

Transfer the cords of the building plan from the corner stakes to nails hammered in the batter boards (fig. 4). Check again the diagonal distance between the intersection of the cords at each corner. Next hammer nails into each 'leg' of the batter boards 3′ (10cm) inside those already set and fix cords between them. Now measure along cord A-B distances of 10′ (3m) and 13′ (3.96m), 20′ (6.09m) and 23′ (7m) and drive stakes into the ground at these points. Repeat this between C-D and attach cords to nails in the top of each stake. You will now have constructed the layout as shown

Fig. 4 Batter board layout

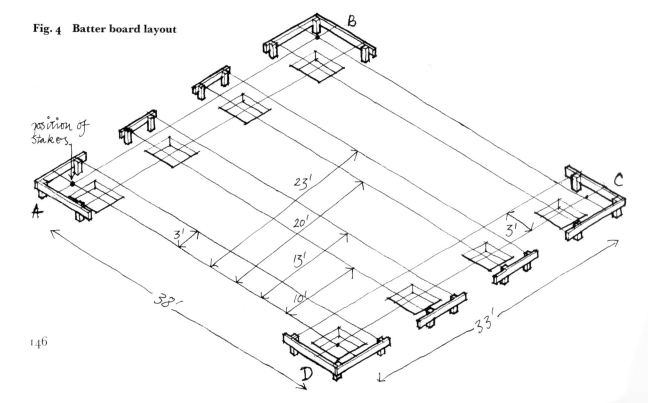

position of stakes

in fig. 4. Where the cords intersect there will be eight 3′ squares. These are the bases for the columns. Run sand over these lines and remove the cords. The squares will show up as clean unsanded lengths on the ground and can now be excavated. At any time the cords can be replaced.

Excavate the column bases to a depth of 2′ (60cm). Measure down from the cords to obtain equal depths in the excavations and ram the bottom with the rammer ready for concrete. Drive a stake in each hole leaving 9″ (23cm) projecting from the base for the concrete thickness. Make sure each is level, using a long straight edge and spirit level. Careful levelling at this stage is essential; the top of the concrete base will correspond exactly with the tops of the stakes and

must be level as the height of the columns and consequently the accuracy of placing the main roof beams depend on it.

Now excavate a trench 1′6″ (46cm) deep for a distance of 15′ (4.5m) from a point half-way along AD and BC of the garden room, for the rainwater drainage (see fig. 5). At the end of the trench excavate a pit 4′ (1m) deep. Fill these pits with rubble or gravel up to 1′ (30cm) from the top for soakaways (drywells). Lay a 3″ (7.5cm) bed of rubble or gravel in the trench and a 4″ (10cm) diameter PVC pipe with a slight fall of about 3″ (7.5cm) leading into the soakaway (drywell). Join a bend to this horizontal pipe and support the short vertical section by placing rubble or gravel around it.

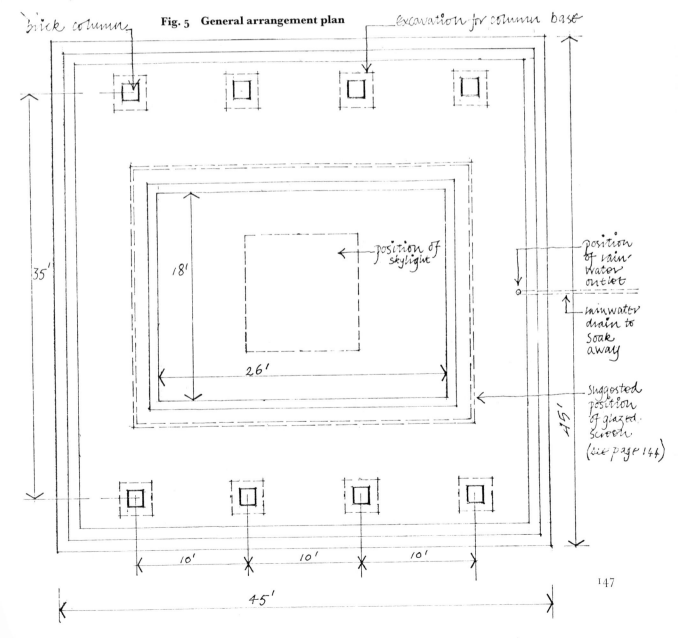

Fig. 5   General arrangement plan

brick column

excavation for column base

position of skylight

18′

26′

35′

position of rainwater outlet

rainwater drain to soakaway

suggested position of glazed screen (see page 144)

45′

10′   10′   10′

45′

Foundations

Mix concrete for the column bases using a 1:2:4 mix. Place the concrete in the excavations and level off to the tops of the stakes. The concrete should be left to harden for four days before you start the brickwork. The concrete should not be laid in freezing conditions or if it is laid in very hot sunny weather it should be covered with sacking to prevent too-rapid setting and possible cracking.

Before laying any bricks, mark the centre of the columns on the concrete bases. Spread mortar 1:3 about $\frac{1}{2}''$ (1.2cm) thick and bed the first course of bricks for each column in the arrangement shown in fig. 6. Lay two further courses and make sure that the joints are well filled with mortar. At this point check with the tape measure that the dimensions are correct between centres of columns. Any minor adjustment can be made in the next few courses. Continue building the columns for a further ten courses or, if you are using a brick thinner than $2\frac{5}{8}''$, the nearest course to $3'3''$ (1m). Always round up to the nearest course. Use the gauge rod to check that the courses are rising correctly and the spirit level to ensure verticality.

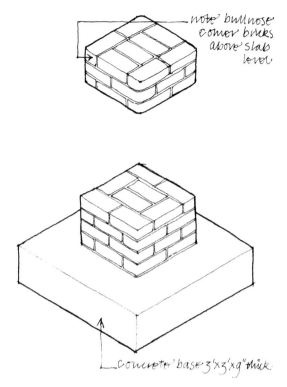

note 'bullnose' corner bricks above slab level

Concrete base 3'x3'x9" thick

Fig. 6   Alternate courses for columns

Forms for central floor slab and inner first step

The wooden forms against which the slab will soon be cast must now be positioned in a rectangle $26' \times 18'$ (8m $\times$ 5.5m) centrally between the grid lines formed by the columns. As there is a considerable amount of wood required for all the forms, and as it is only to be used once, you may try to hire it from a specialist form contractor. If not, secondhand wood should be used. Nail the boards securely to stout $2'' \times 2''$ (5cm $\times$ 5cm) stakes driven firmly into the ground as shown in fig. 8. Where a joint occurs between form boards there should be a stake at each end of the adjoining boards. The stakes must be long enough to carry first of all the formwork for the central floor slab, and later the boards for the first inner step.

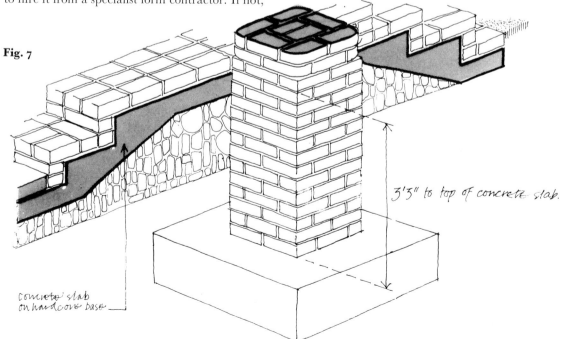

Fig. 7

3'3" to top of concrete slab.

concrete slab on hardcore base

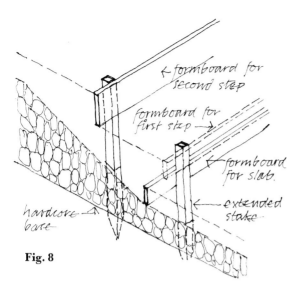

Fig. 8

Care in laying out is essential; you must check frequently with the spirit level along the top edge of each board and make sure the stakes are vertical. Time spent in ensuring that this is done correctly will avoid difficulties later. A 2″ (5cm) polythene tube for the future electrical installation should be laid at this stage.

Base for floor slab

Lay a 6″ thickness of hardcore (or gravel) within this area, ramming it well to ensure that it is well compacted, and finish off with a 2″ (5cm) layer of sand or ash to fill any spaces between the pieces and give a smooth level bed.

Laying the floor slab

First divide the floor slab area between the forms into two halves with a 1″ × 4″ (2.5cm × 10cm) board (or boards) wedged against the perimeter boards and levelled. It must be securly fixed and should be rigid.

Now the concrete can be poured into one half of the divided floor area. It should be laid initially so that it is slightly higher than the forms and then,

using the board edges as a guide, tamp the concrete using a 'sawing' and tamping motion. Any hollows, no matter how slight, must be filled as you go.

When the concrete has hardened, remove the temporary boards and repeat for the second half.

Forms for the raised area and remaining steps

In general the comments and description of the forms for the central floor slab apply equally to that for the steps and raised area. Further explanation can also be found on pages 52-5 in the section on steps.

Careful laying out is vital. As a guide for erecting the forms for the steps lay cords and long stakes where the front of each board will be; they will be at varying heights to correspond with the height of the steps. Make sure the stakes are driven firmly into the ground, particularly those which are to form the top steps as they have to support the weight of a large volume of wet concrete. Nail form boards along the stakes. The long stakes used in casting the central floor slab will now serve also to carry forms for the first inner step.

The stakes should be nailed at no more than 2′6″ (76.2cm) intervals. Any point where two boards abut there should be a stake each side of the join. Check the level of the tops of each board with the spirit level, adjust as necessary and check the dimensions between the boards. It is a good idea to re-check with the square that each corner is a true right-angle. It may be helpful to reinforce the formwork by nailing a batten between the parallel boards.

Before pouring the concrete, coat the surface of the wood against which the concrete will be cast with liquid detergent or a proprietary form release oil. This will make removal of the forms much easier.

Fig. 9   Arrangement detail of column and stepped slab

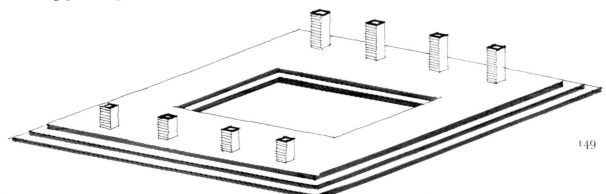

The raised area and steps

You must build up the level under the raised area with hardcore (or gravel). Lay this in layers of 6″ (15cm): lay one 6″ (15cm) layer, ram it well to fill all voids and then lay another 6″ (15cm) layer. Build up the hardcore (or gravel) in this way sloping off the side areas which will be under the steps until it is 1′6″ (45.7cm) thick, and then face with 2″ (5cm) sand. Check that the forms have not been knocked out of place.

Laying the concrete. Ready-mixed concrete or a mechanical mixer is essential for the amount of concrete needed here. The mix should be 1:2:4 as before. Start by laying the bottom step on each side, tamping the concrete with a short length of 1″ × 4″ (2.5cm × 10cm) wood using the bottom edge of the form board as the guide. Next repeat this for the next steps. You will have to transport the concrete over the raised area. Provide a runway using large boards to get over the forms and into the centre. Allow the concrete to harden and then lay more concrete for the third outside step and complete by laying the concrete for the flat raised area, tamping it across the two top boards.

Leave the forms in place for at least seven days before striking (removing).

Columns

Back now to the brickwork. Lay the courses (in the same bond pattern as before but this time use a 1:1:6 mortar mix and use the single bullnose facing bricks for the corners (fig. 10). Then spread ⅜″ (1cm) thickness of mortar and lay any damp-proof course. This can be either heavy black PVC or a bituminous non-organic felt (see page 33). It should be 1′6″ (45cm) wide. If you cannot buy it this width, use three pieces 9″ (23cm) wide and overlap each piece. Spread a mortar bed on top of this and continue building up the columns using expanded metal reinforcement ties every fourth course; two 8″ wide strips about 1′3″ long should be used. Check frequently with the spirit level to ensure that the columns are vertical and use the gauge rod to check that your brickwork is rising correctly. Build the columns up to 7′9″ from the top of the concrete floor slab for the raised area.

Six courses from the top leave out the centre bricks but build up the outside bricks with 4½″

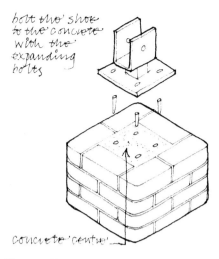

bolt the shoe to the concrete with the expanding bolts

concrete centre

Fig. 10 Detail of top of columns

(11cm) wide strips of expanded metal projecting about 2″ (5cm) into the void. To reinforce the column, fill this void with concrete up to the top of the column, covering the metal strips (fig. 10).

Flush point all the vertical joints between the bricks with coloured cement to match the bricks. When this has begun to harden, recess the horizontal joints about ¼″ (6mm) but no more than ⅜″ (1cm). See page 38 for detailed general information on pointing. Check that the tops of all columns are level and position the steel shoes. Mark the holes and drill the concrete for the depth of the bolt sockets. Insert the sockets and bolt down the shoes, inserting lead sheet packing beneath the plates if necessary to level the shoes.

Roof: fixing the main beams

To position each of the main beams you will need two portable scaffold towers placed adjacent to each pair of columns in turn, and a rig with lifting tackle midway between the columns. Place the box beams alongside the pairs of columns and with the help of friends attach the lifting tackle using a rope cradle around the centre of the beam. Raise it, guiding to prevent swing and gently lower the beam into the shoes. Repeat for all four beams making sure that the ends are level. Drill the side of the beam through the holes in the shoe and bolt with the ⅜″ (1cm) diameter bolts.

Next attach the curved steel holding-down ties (see fig. 3c). Hold them in position and mark the columns where the holes occur. Drill the brickwork and insert the 'shell' of the rawlbolt. Bolt the ties to the brickwork and coach screw the top to the underside of the beams.

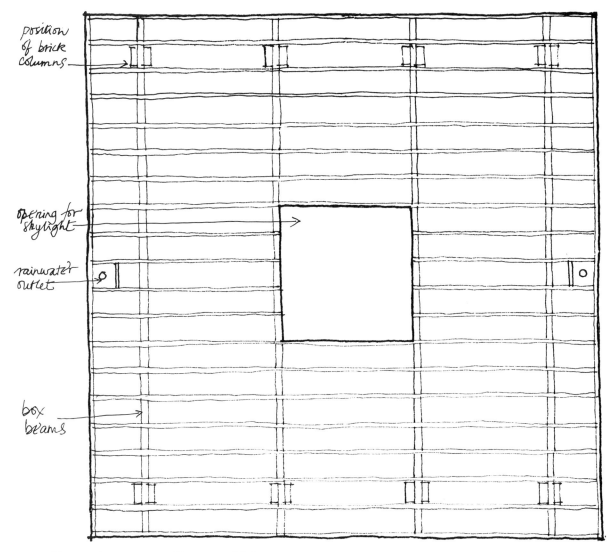

position of brick columns

opening for skylight

rainwater outlet

box beams

Fig. 11   Arrangment of beams and joists

Fig. 12   Detail of joists nailed to main beams

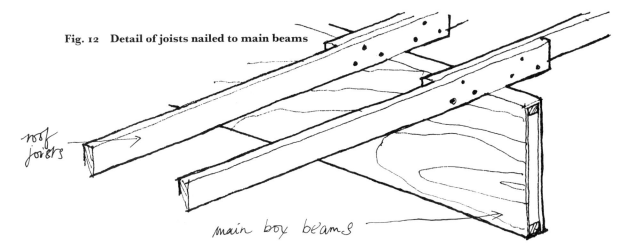

roof joists

main box beams

Roof joists

Mark the centrepoint of each of the main box beams with a crayon and working out from this, position the $2'' \times 6''$ (5cm × 15cm) wooden joists at right-angles to the main beams at $2'$ (60cm) centres. Measure a $4'$ (1m) overhang to ensure that the ends are level and leave a central opening for the rooflight as shown in fig 11. Again, wood is not generally available in such lengths and the separate lengths should be lapped over the centre beams and nailed together (fig. 12). The separate lengths can be pre-cut—$15'6''$ (4.7m) for the outer and $12'$ (3.7m) for centre joists. Nail the joists to the top of the box beams using $6''$ (15cm) oval nails driven at an angel through the joists from each side. Nail $2'' \times 6''$ (5cm × 15cm) wood as a trimmer for the skylight.

Gussets, roof decking, and rainwater outlet

To give the soffit its characteristic curved form, cut the gussets from $\frac{3}{4}''$ (2cm) thick plywood. As 244 of these are required you may prefer to avoid the drudgery of cutting them by making a full size drawing and taking it to a specialist wood worker who will have the machinery to mass-produce them. If you decide to have the gussets made in this way, you can have them drilled with four $\frac{3}{32}''$ (2.4mm) holes for nailing to the joists otherwise you will have to do this yourself. Nail the gussets to the joists and main beams (fig 13).

The finished roof must have falls, i.e. a slope so that rainwater can run off and not sit in pools.

To achieve this and give a fall of $1\frac{1}{2}''$ (3.7cm) in $10'$ (3m) you will have to make 'firring pieces'. These are long pieces of wood tapered and nailed along the joists with the highest point at the centre of the roof, then falling to the edges (fig. 14). To make them, cut lengths of $2''$ (5cm) wood $7'6''$ (2.2m) long to a point, so that some pieces are tapered from $3''$ (7.6cm) down to $1\frac{1}{2}''$ (3.7cm) and some from $1\frac{1}{2}''$ (3.7cm) down to zero and nail these along the joists with the highest point in the centre of the roof.

Next lay $2''$ (5cm) glass fibre quilt for insulation over the top of the joists and firrings and nail $\frac{1}{2}''$ (1.2cm) plywood sheets $4' \times 8'$ (1.2m × 2.4m) as roof decking. The sheets should be laid with the length of the sheet across the joists and should be staggered, with the shortest edge lying over a joist

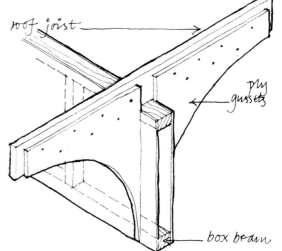

Fig. 13 Nailing the gussets to joists and main beams

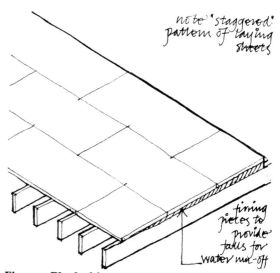

Fig. 14 Ply decking arrangement

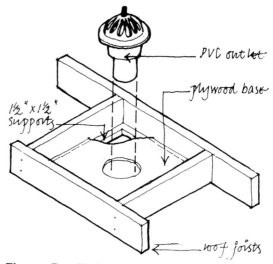

Fig. 15 Detail of rainwater outlet

(fig. 14). Nail the sheets with $1\frac{1}{4}''$ (3.2cm) oval nails at 1′ (30cm) centres to each joist. Punch the nail heads below the surface and don't cover the opening in the centre for the skylight.

Before completing the roof decking, make a box for the rainwater outlets at each side of the garden room. Nail cross members between two joists in the position shown in fig 11. Position the outlet by dropping a plumb-line directly over the rainwater drainage pipe in the concrete slab below. The outlet must be directly over the drainage pipes as later we will be placing aluminium rainwater pipes between them. Fix $1\frac{1}{2}'' \times 1\frac{1}{2}''$ (3.7cm × 3.7cm) wooden supports to the sides of the box (fig. 15) and nail a plywood square with a $3\frac{1}{2}''$ (9cm) drain hole cut in the centre for the outlet. Inside the box nail $1\frac{1}{2}'' \times 1\frac{1}{2}''$ (3.7cm × 3.7cm) wooden angle fillet for the roofing felt to be dressed over. Complete the plywood decking.

Skylight upstand
Nail a $2'' \times 4''$ (5cm × 10cm) upstand around the opening of the skylight with $1\frac{1}{2}'' \times 1\frac{1}{2}''$ (3.7cm × 3.7cm) fillet nailed around the perimeter to avoid sharp right-angles. line the opening with

$\frac{1}{2}''$ (1.2cm) plywood for a neat finish.

The glassed skylight will be a manufactured item. It can be fibreglass or glass in an aluminium framing and will usually be fixed after the roof covering is laid. The upstand will give an adequate bearing for most types. We suggest that the skylight be pyramid-shaped.

Edge upstand and fascia
All around the edge of the roof nail an upstand made from $2'' \times 4''$ (5cm × 10cm) wood with one $2''$ (5cm) edge chamfered to a 45° angle, laid flat and nailed through to the joists with $4''$ (10cm) nails (fig. 17).

Cut the fascia from $\frac{3}{4}''$ (2cm) marine ply. You will need 10′ (3m) sheets to cut from so that the joints coincide with the centres between main beams. The bottom edge should be 1″ (2.5cm) below the joists to mask the edge of the soffit boarding. To get a smooth surface, fix $1'' \times 2''$ (2.5cm × 5cm) runners top and bottom of the roof joists; when fixing these check with the spirit level that they are perfectly level, pack out if necessary behind them to achieve this. Provide runners in a similar way along the two sides where the ends of

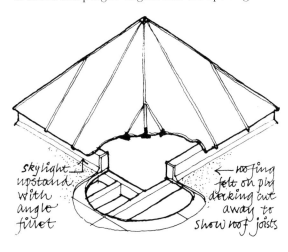

Fig. 16   Skylight detail

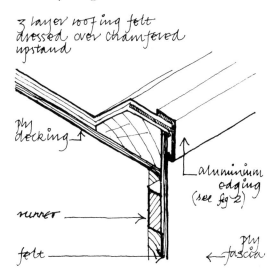

Fig. 17   Eaves (detail of 18)

the joists are projecting; nail them to the end of the joists.

Fix a layer of bituminous felt vertically behind the fascia. This will prevent water which enters the joints between the fascia panels from running back into the roof space (fig. 18).

Drill and countersink the plywood for the fascia and screw to the runners with brass screws. Stop up the holes with wood filler and sand down flush before painting. See fig. 19 for dimensions of fascia panels.

Fig. 18   Detail of roof/fascia build-up

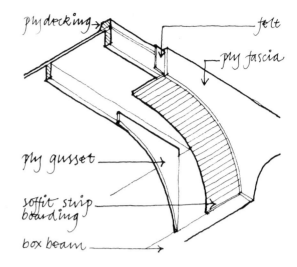

Fig 19   Fascia panels

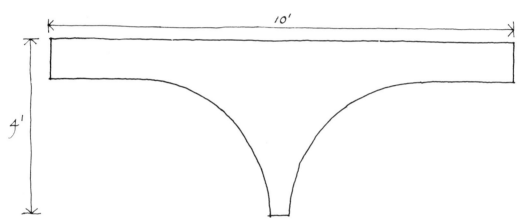

Roof covering

The roof is now ready for covering. We suggest you have this work carried out by a roofing specialist who may also supply the PVC rainwater outlets. You should specify two layers of inorganic bituminous felt roofing laid over a perforated breather sheathing and finishing with $\frac{1}{2}''$ (1.2cm) granite chippings laid on the top surface. Make sure that the edge trim shown in fig. 1 is a purpose-made extruded aluminium section. This will give a neat finish to the roof edge.

Next attach the rainwater pipes. These are $4''$ (10cm) diameter aluminium pipes running in one length from the outlet to the drainage pipe below. They will be unsupported except at the top and bottom and it is important to make sure that the connections are not loose and the top secured with a pipe clip screwed to the joists.

Ceiling

Board the ceiling using a planed wooden $\frac{3}{4}'' \times 1\frac{1}{2}''$ (2cm × 3.7cm) square-edged wood strip nailed to the soffit of the joists. This should follow the curve and continue vertically to the bottom edge of the plywood box beams.

Suitable wood would be redwood or cedar coated with a colourless matt lacquer for a natural finish.

If cedar is used, make sure that the pins to fix the strips are non-ferrous, or staining may occur. Discuss the detailing of the window joinery with a specialist. Ideally the framing at ceiling level should be concealed, with the ceiling finish stopping on either side of the glass line for an apparently continuous finish.

Electrical installation

Call in the electrician to lay power supply cables and provide floor socket outlets for power and lighting which will be by floor lamps.

Floor screed

Paint the concrete slab for the 'sunken' area with two coats of a bituminous compound for a damp-proof membrane. Call in a specialist to lay a 2½" (6cm) thick cement-sand screed. Protect this after it has been laid until all the building work, including painting, is completed.

Painting

There is very little painting. Use clear lacquer for the boarded ceiling, applying a minimum of two coats, and three coats of brown or black stain, for the plywood fascia. Don't use dark coloured paint; it will absorb heat from the sun and blister and peel very quickly.

Laying the bricks for the steps and raised area

Before you begin, read about steps on pages 52-5 and pavings on pages 58-77.

Start laying the bricks on the top step. Mark the centre of the length of the step and work outwards to each corner. Bed the bricks on edge in mortar 1:1:6. Lift a full trowel of mortar and lay on the concrete step; next 'butter' the brick on one side with mortar and place down on the mortar bed, tapping into place with the trowel handle.

Form the risers to the steps by using two courses of brick bedded in mortar as shown in fig 7. When laying, make sure that the joints line through. Do this for all three sets of steps on each side of the raised area, working in sequence from the top step to the bottom. Flush joint as the work proceeds and clean off surplus mortar from the brick face.

Lay the paving to the raised area in stack bond (jack-on-jack). Bed the bricks in mortar on the concrete with the joints well filled; flush joint and clean off surplus mortar from the bricks as you go. When you get to the corners of each step the bricks can either be laid mitre cut (see page 55) or butted.

Fig. 20   Section

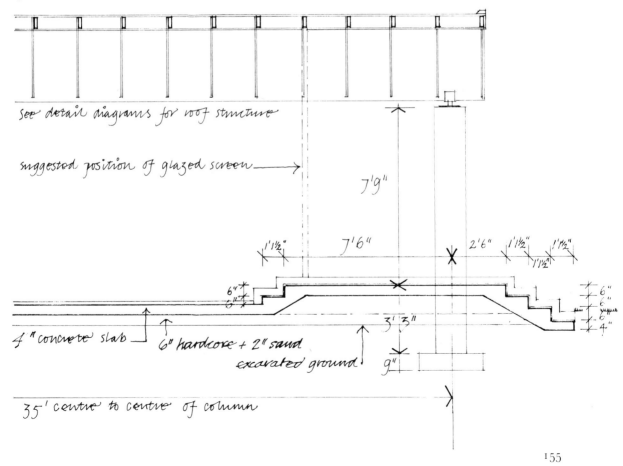

see detail diagrams for roof structure

suggested position of glazed screen ⟶

7'9"

1'1½"   7'6"   2'6"   1'1½"   1'1½"   1'1½"

6"
6"

6"
6"
6"
4"

4" concrete slab

6" hardcore + 2" sand

excavated ground   9"

3'3"

35' centre to centre of column

Indoor furniture

Brick is not just an outdoor material: there are just as many possibilities for using brick indoors as there are outdoors. One thing you are not concerned with is resistance to weather, and so just about any kind of brick can be used so long as the colour and texture matches with the rest of the interior. Low tables like our design can be built as coffee-tables in a sitting room, or, combined with one of the shelving systems, could help create a cosy study. The general principle can be adapted fairly easily to suit many situations and you could even think up your own design without much effort. Basically the building principle is the same as for a low wall. A small indoor planter and table combined would be quite the thing, now that everyone is house-plant mad. Or your table could be painted with any colour of paint if you want to build it cheaply with common bricks which are not very beautiful. The whole appearance of the table could be changed as quickly as it takes to apply another coat.

Anyone who loves books likes to show them off to advantage by providing nicely designed shelving for them. We have designed two different kinds; the first is entirely adaptable—new piers and shelves can be built quickly and easily and you can alter the heights of the shelves as you wish. The second design is a little more sophisticated and not quite as adaptable and so for the avid reader who keeps running out of space, the first design will probably be more suitable.

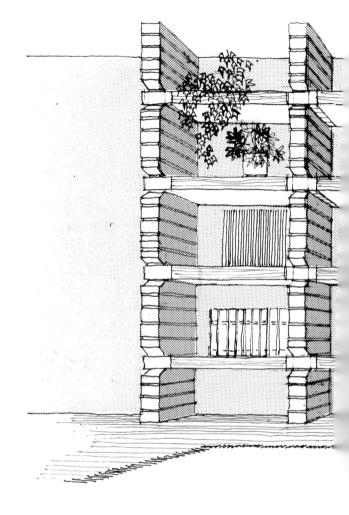

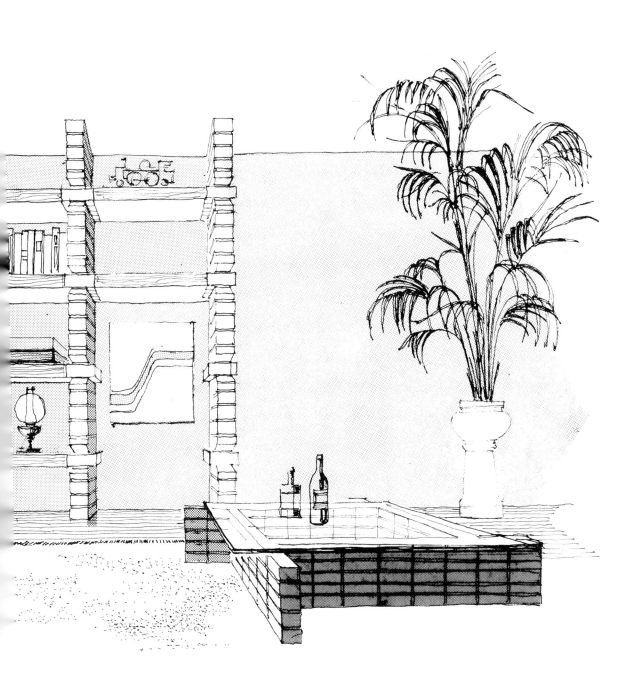

Shelving system 1.

This shelving system is simple but requires a good deal of care. Pay attention to the brick piers; they must be straight and carefully laid. This applies to all brickwork of course, but this project is going to be seen at close range and any imperfections will show up more clearly.

Your choice of brick is very important. The bricks should have a similar colour and texture on both sides. We use double-bullnose bricks to give a neat finish to the piers and this will restrict your choice to a range that includes them. If you find them difficult to buy, or prohibitively expensive, you could use ordinary bricks. Also consider the room itself: will the colour of your bricks complement the carpet, furniture etc?

You must also consider the type of floor. There will be no problem if this is a solid concrete slab but if it consists of joists and boards then the brick piers must be built against a wall which has the boards running up to it. This will ensure that the brickwork is supported by two joists running at right-angles and is not simply built on the floor boarding alone.

We will describe how to build four piers and three bays.

You can build as many piers as you have space for but they should not be further apart than 3′ (90cm) from the centre of one pier to the centre of the next. This will ensure that quite heavy objects can be put on the shelves.

The shelves are carried on hollow rectangular steel tubes which fit into slots in the brick piers and are adjustable for height in 'one brick' increments.

Tools

You will need all the basic tools listed on page 25 plus:
Right-angle square
Steel tape-measure
Gauge rod

Materials

The materials listed are sufficient for three bays of shelving, i.e. four brick piers 6′6″ high and 15 shelves.

You should use standard-sized solid bricks

200 facing bricks
150 double-bullnose bricks (or ordinary bricks)
15 shelves made from $\frac{3}{4}″ \times 1′2\frac{1}{2}″$ (2cm × 37.5cm) hardwood or melamine laminate veneered blockboard 2′6″ (76cm) long.
Note: the strips forming the core of the blockboard should run the length of the shelf, and veneered boards should have a veneer on both sides.

15 Finished 'half-round' edging strips actual size $2′6″ \times 2\frac{1}{4}″ \times 2″$ (76cm × 5.6cm × 5cm)
$\frac{3}{4}″ \times 1\frac{1}{2}″$ (2cm × 3.7cm) hardwood
30 lengths expanded metal ties
13yds (12m) rectangular hollow steel tubing
glue (PVA)
mortar (see estimating table). Use coloured cement to match the bricks 1:1:6 mix

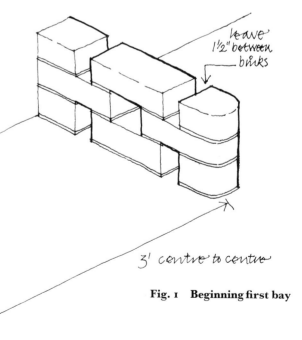

leave 1½″ between bricks

3′ centre to centre

bullnose bricks

Fig. 1   Beginning first bay

Piers

If you have a solid slab floor, take up the floor finish where the shelving system is to be built and mark out the positions of the piers with chalk at 3′ (90cm) centre to centre. Mark the wall as well with a vertical line at the same points. Screw a strip of expanded metal 3″ (7.5cm) or 4″ (10cm) wide and about 8″ (20cm) long at 5′ (1.5m) and 6′ (1.8m) from the floor to provide a tie to the top of each pier (fig. 2). Spread $\frac{1}{2}$″ (1.2cm) of mortar on the floor and lay the first course of bricks stretcher (running) bond in the arrangement shown in fig. 1, i.e. one half-brick against the wall, then on full brick, then a half-bullnose, with $1\frac{1}{2}$″ (3.7cm) space between each brick. Clean out any mortar from between the bricks. Lay the second and following courses always leaving the $1\frac{1}{2}$″ (3.7cm) space and cutting the mortar off flush with the bricks as you go.

If your floor is boarded, follow the same method but set out the system in such a way that the brickwork will be at right-angles to the joists and bond the first course of bricks to the floor with epoxy resin.

Shelves

When you have had the boards cut to size, the shelves will need very little work. Simply glue the edging to the long edge of each shelf using a PVA adhesive, clamp until set and then carefully sand and polish. The important thing to remember is that, for best effect, the surface of each shelf should be absolutely smooth and flush with the edging.

Screw a triangular wooden blocking strip to the underside of each shelf to reinforce the joint between the edging and the shelf and help to reduce shrinkage cracks (fig. 3).

Finally, slot the steel tube bearers through the open joints in the brickwork and position the shelves.

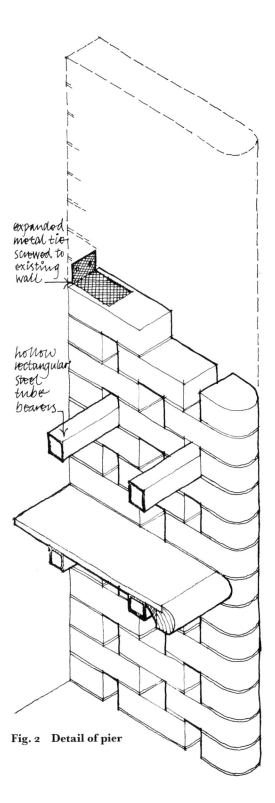

expanded metal tie screwed to existing wall

hollow rectangular steel tube bearers

Fig. 2   Detail of pier

Fig. 3   Detail of shelf

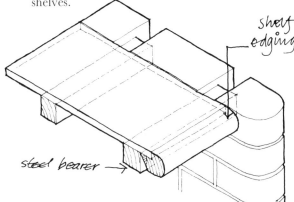

shelf edging

steel bearer →

Shelving system 2.

This shelving system is similar in principle to the one described on the previous page. Although it has a different appearance and a slightly more detailed shelving arrangement, the general remarks concerning the choice of bricks, colour etc., and type of floor will apply here as well.

The main difference is that the shelves are supported on projecting bricks built into the piers and are carried by anodized aluminium angle bearers. This system is quite substantial but will not carry objects that are very heavy. It is suitable for books and most other domestic uses.

It is important to glue a piece of $1'' \times 2''$ (2.5cm × 5cm) wood to the underside of the shelf at each end to hold the screws for the angle bearers. If this is omitted then the screw fixings will be in the end-grain of the wood; this is a weak fixing for screws and they may come out after a time. The shelves in this system are not as adjustable for height to the same extent as system 1.

Tools

You will need all the basic tools listed on page 25 plus:
Right-angle square
Steel tape-measure
Gauge rod

Materials

The materials listed are sufficient for three bays of shelving, i.e., four brick piers 6′6″ high and 15 shelves.

You should use standard-sized solid bricks.
250 facing bricks
100 plinth headers (or ordinary bricks)
15 shelves made from $\frac{3}{4}'' \times 1'2\frac{1}{2}''$ (2cm × 37.5cm) hardwood or melamine laminate veneered blockboard 2′6″ (76cm) long

Note: the strips which form the core of the blockboard must run the length of the shelf. Veneered boards should have a veneer on both sides.

15 $1\frac{1}{8}'' \times 2\frac{5}{8}''$ (2.8cm × 6.7cm) hardwood edging strips, 2′6″ (76cm) long
30 $2'' \times 2\frac{1}{2}''$ (5cm × 7.2cm) anodized aluminium angle bearers 1′4″ (40.6cm) long
expanded metal ties
$1\frac{1}{4}''$ (3cm) screws for the shelves
glue (PVA)
Mortar (see estimating table) use coloured cement to match the bricks 1:1:6 mix

Fig. 4   Beginning first bay

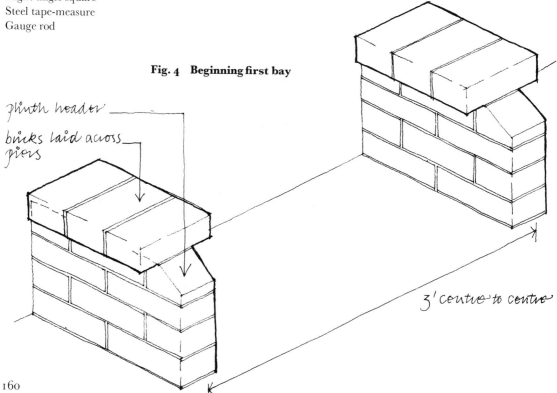

plinth header

bricks laid across piers

3′ centre to centre

Piers

Follow the same method exactly as described on pages 158-9 for system 1, but lay the bricks in the formation shown in fig. 4 and do not leave a 1″ space between each brick. Build up four courses for each pier with a plinth header at the front on each fourth course. Then lay three full bricks across the piers bedding each in mortar with the vertical joints between flushed up. Lay the straight-edge and spirit level across each pier in turn to check that they are horizontal. These projecting bricks must be level as they support the shelves.

At the front of the sixth course and after every course of projecting bricks, put a plinth header inverted as shown in fig. 5.

Build up the piers in this way to your required height (no higher than 8′ [2.4m]).

The shelves

Glue and clamp a 1″ × 2″ (2.5cm × 5cm) planed wooden strip to the underside of the ends of each shelf. This will hold the screws for the bearers.

Glue the edging strip to the long edge of each shelf with a PVA wood adhesive. Screw a triangular wooden blocking strip to the underside of each shelf to reinforce the joint between the edging and the shelf and help reduce shrinkage cracks. Carefully smooth the edging, making sure of a flush finish between the top of the board and the edging.

Next drill the aluminium angle to take the screws and countersink the holes. The holes should be halfway down the longest leg of the angle at 6″ (15cm) centres except at the front edge where it is advisable to screw-fix twice, $\frac{1}{2}$″ (1.2cm) and 2″ (5cm) from the bottom edge of the angle (fig. 6).

Polish the edging strip and position the shelves, resting them on the projecting brick courses.

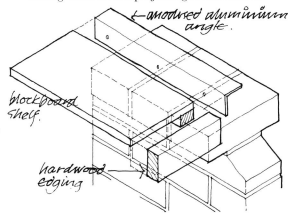

← anodised aluminium angle.

blockboard shelf.

hardwood edging

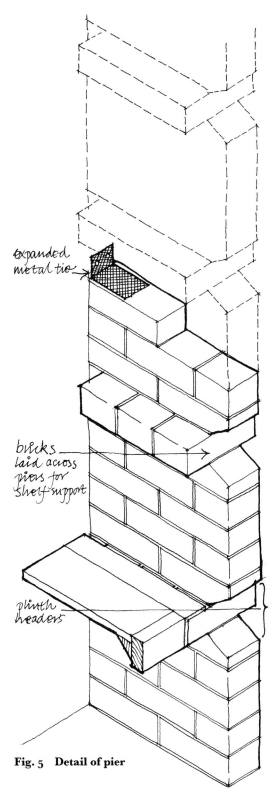

expanded metal tie

bricks laid across piers for shelf support

plinth headers

Fig. 5 Detail of pier

Fig. 6 Detail of shelf

Table

This table is designed for indoor use; it can be built in your living room, garden room or wherever you like. It will be quite solid and you wont be able to move it around, so you must take care to choose a good position for it in the room. It is simple and quick to build and can be taken down and rebuilt with little inconvenience.

Although it would be rather impractical to build it on fitted carpets, most other types of floor finish would be fine. To protect the existing floor finish you should lay 4″ (10cm) wide strips of expanded metal on the floor and bed the first course of bricks in mortar on this. This will prevent damage or staining occurring if you wish to re-arrange the room at some future date.

Tools
You will need all the basic tools listed on page 25 plus:
Right-angle square
Gauge rod

Materials
You should use standard-sized solid bricks.
120 bricks
8 galvanized wire cavity wall ties
4 strips ¼″ (6mm) thick expanded metal 4″ (10cm) wide and 4′6″ (1.4m) long.
4 rubber door stops with screws.
1 sheet plate glass ¾″ (2cm) thickness 4′ (1.2m) square
Mortar (see estimating table) 1:1:6 mix
Polythene sheet

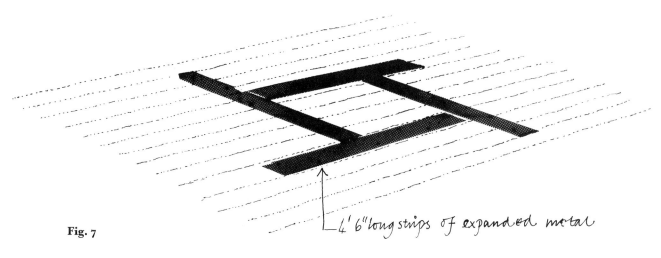

4′6″ long strips of expanded metal

Fig. 7

You have a fairly wide choice of bricks for your table; they should have a similar colour and texture on all faces which, generally speaking, excludes most mechanically textured or sand-faced. Most important is that they should complement the colour scheme of the room. To achieve this you could buy an inexpensive common brick and cover with emulsion paint; this would be very effective and has the added advantage of being easily changed.

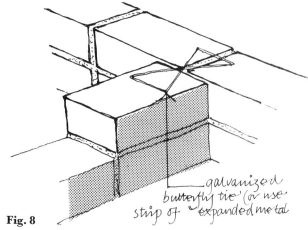

galvanized butterfly tie (or use strip of expanded metal

Fig. 8

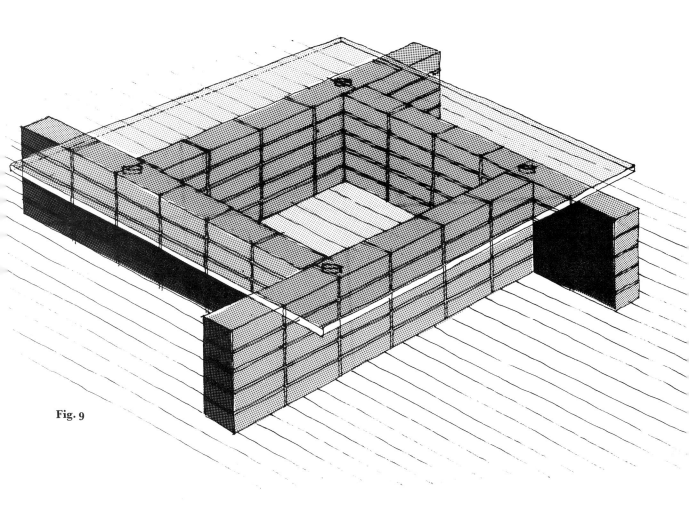

Fig. 9

Building the base

Decide on position for the table and lay a sheet of polythene about 6′ (1.8m) square to protect the existing floor finish from mortar droppings. The polythene can be trimmed off afterwards. Lay the strips of expanded metal on the floor (fig. 7). Drill four small holes in each strip and nail to the floor using small, tough steel masonry nails if you have a solid floor or panel pins if you have a wooden floor. Before nailing the strips down check with the right-angle square to make sure that they are accurately positioned.

Spread $\frac{1}{2}″$ (1.2cm) mortar on the expanded metal and bed the first course of bricks on the mortar, 'buttering' the header of each brick to make sure all the vertical joints are well filled with mortar. Build each brick ring using six bricks five courses high with the galvanized ties at the second and fourth course. Lay the bricks with vertical joints directly over one another.

Strike a flush joint with the edge of the trowel blade. Trim off the polythene sheet so that none remains visible and finally, when the mortar has hardened, say four to five days, drill the brick, insert plastic plugs and screw the rubber door stops.

If you wish, paint the brickwork with two coats of emulsion paint when it has thoroughly dried out. Black, dark brown or white are probably the most appropriate choices. Place the plate glass top on the rubber door stops and your table is complete.

Fireplace

Most of the previous projects have concentrated on outdoor use, but the principles covered in the first basic chapters apply equally well to indoor bricklaying. Don't imagine that bricks are only for your garden or exterior walls—more and more decorators appreciate the marvellous impact brick walls and constructions can create in antique or modern homes. Bricks can blend perfectly with other natural textures—long-pile rugs, rough-finished planking or barn siding, deep-woven tweeds, or hand-sewn beams, and will contrast with the glow of centuries-old wood polished to a deep shine, soft velvet cushions, silk hangings, or the scrolled outline of an ormolu-framed mirror.

For the complete beginner, it is better to start bricklaying with a small outdoor project before tackling something indoors—mistakes can be rectified more easily outdoors or covered with trailing greenery. For outdoors as long as the bricks blend in tone with your house, they need not be any special colour. But indoor work calls for a little more exactness. The joints should be finer, and more carefully pointed, the bricks themselves carefully chosen for the room. This is one project where it is worth-while making a trip to your local brickyard or merchant, to choose from the wide variety of textures and colours. If you already have upholstery and carpets, take along swatches—it is surprising how the pink or red in a print can be affected by a just-right or a just-wrong tone in the brick wall you are planning. Remember too that there will be quite a lot of wall! For some indoor work, it may be better to choose a hand-cut mottled colour which has a softer effect; machine-made solid colour bricks are fine in small doses, but tend to be overpowering in large quantities. And don't be afraid to ask for sample bricks to take home—light conditions will affect the colours more indoors than outside, and most brick merchants will be delighted to help you become a steady and satisfied customer!

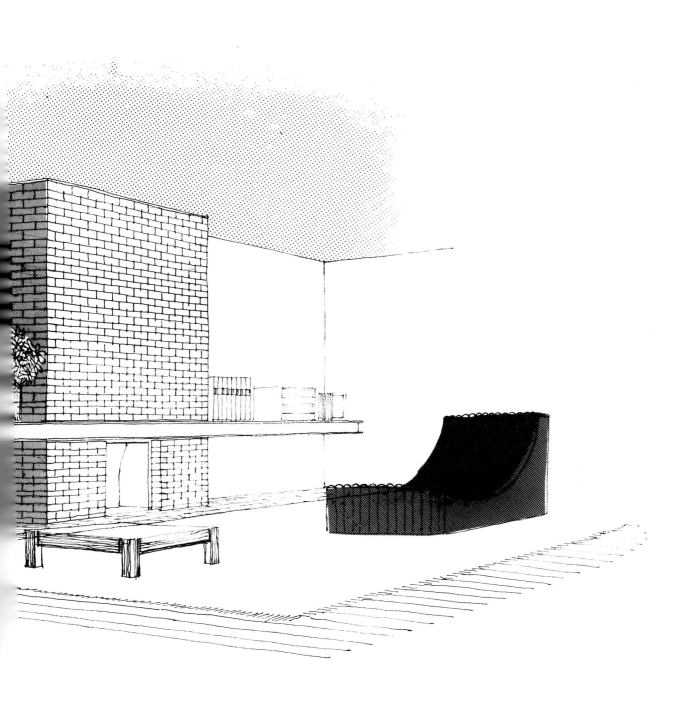

Getting started.

This project is fairly simple and it can change the character of a room allowing you to make a feature of an uninteresting chimney breast. Perhaps the fireplace has a rather dull tiled slab fire-surround which, because of its importance as a focal point, prevents modernization anywhere else in the room. Of course, if your room has a pretty or interesting old fireplace you may not wish to change it but if you do, then this project will make an attractive and dramatic change to the room.

Our project is designed as a brick skin 'wrapped' around your old chimney breast with two side alcoves. The existing chimney breast will have its own concrete slab hearth which will support the new outer brick skin, but there are limitations regarding the side 'wing' consisting of two alcoves: it can only be built on a solid concrete slab floor. A boarded floor on wooden joists will not bear the weight of the new brickwork, so make sure of this before you begin.

Decide on the kind of 'look' you want in the room, whether rugged or smoothly sophisticated, for instance, and choose a type of brick to help you achieve this. Ideally the brick should have a similar colour and texture on each face as our design has dividing piers which are seen from both sides. The colour will be important as well: clay bricks come in any colour from white to almost black, but use very dark bricks with caution; they can look too over-powering in a fairly small room.

The design calls for a rolled steel channel which if possible should be sand-blasted before delivery for a smooth finish. You could clean it off to a bright finish with power tools.

Tools

You will need all the basic tools listed on page 25 plus:
Right-angle square

Materials

The quantities of bricks and the length of the steel channel required will depend on your individual chimney breast. Calculate the numbers of facing bricks allowing 48 bricks per sq yd (54 per m³).

Here we will assume a chimney breast 4′6″ (1.4m) wide × 1′6″ (46cm) deep and room height of 8′ (2.4m). For this you will need:
750 facing bricks (use standard-sized solid bricks).

6 sq yds (5m²) of quarry tiles or paving bricks
6″ × 3″ (15cm × 7.5cm) rolled steel channel 15′ (4.6m) long with a 1″ × 1″ (2.5cm × 2.5cm) steel angle shelf support welded to the back (fig. 8).
Note: The channel should be 1″ (2.5cm) less than the overall length of the brickwork.
1 roll of 6″ (10cm) wide expanded metal mesh for ties.
1″ (2.5cm) melamine-faced blockboard for shelf.
Mortar (see estimating table) 1:1:6 mix

Removing the old fireplace

The first step is to remove the old fireplace surround and hearth. If they are the tiled slab sort, they will be quite heavy and you will need someone to help you. Prize it away from the cement jointings with a tool like a crow-bar. Inspect the old fire back carefully; you will probably be able to re-use it, unless it is badly cracked. There may be an existing steel 'trim' to the opening which can also be re-used.

Any existing fire opening is sure to be of a standard size. If the fire back needs replacing you will be able to get one from your local supplier. They usually come in three sections: a back and two sides and they need to be bedded in special fire-cement.

The next step is to cut out slots in the existing brick joints for the expanded metal ties which will tie the new brickwork to the structural wall. To expose the brickwork and locate the joints you will have to hack off some of the old plaster; it should not be necessary to hack it all away. When you

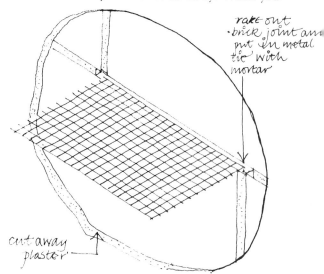

rake out brick joint and put in metal tie with mortar

cut away plaster

Fig. 1

have located the first few brick joints the others can be located by measuring the brick courses. Mark off on the wall the positions for the ties. They will be needed at intervals of about 3′ (90cm) apart horizontally and 1′6″ (45cm) vertically, preferably staggered. Accuracy is not vital. Cut the slots with the brick set and hammer; they should be about 3″ (7.5cm) deep and 6″ (15cm) wide (fig. 2). Push the 6″ (15cm) strips of expanded metal into the slots to protrude about 3″ (7.5cm), mix a quantity of mortar 1:3 and fill up all the space around the metal ties so they will be firmly attached to the existing brickwork when the mortar has set in a couple of days.

The brickwork

Before starting to lay the bricks, check with the spirit level to make sure that the existing wall-face is vertical. If not, you can make the necessary adjustments with the new brickwork. For example, if the existing wall leans into the room slightly, position the first row of bricks away from the wall at the bottom.

Take up the floor finish on either side of the fireplace where the new tiled hearth will be; it should extend a minimum of 1′4″ (40cm) in front of the fire opening. Check the width of the chimney breast. For the bonding to work correctly it should be multiples of the bed depth of your brick. If this is not so, set out the new brick facing to your brick size by leaving a space between the inside of the facing and the sides of the chimney

breast. If you don't set out in this way you may build a 'zipper' into the new brickwork which will look very unpleasant (fig. 2). Mix the mortar 1:1:6. Spread this about ½″ (1.2cm) thick on the floor Making up any obvious discrepancies in level caused by taking up the hearth slab and floor finish. Start from each corner. Lay the first course of bricks, bedding them in the mortar and making sure the joints between and the back of each brick are well filled. Continue laying bricks in stretcher (running) bond as shown in fig. 3, working outwards from each corner. Check with the spirit level to make sure that the brickwork is level and vertical. Cut off the mortar flush with the bricks and try to avoid smearing the face of the brickwork. As the brickwork reaches the ties previously positioned in the existing brickwork, build them into the new facing. Build up to the top of the fire opening and then bed the steel channel in mortar on the bricks and check that it is level. Spread mortar on the top of the channel and continue laying the bricks as before (fig. 4).

When you get to the ceiling, you may find that there is not enough space left at the top for a full course of bricks. In this case, make up the space with a wooden strip wedged between the ceiling and the brickwork (fig. 5). Set the edge of the wood recessed back 1″ (2.5cm) from the brick face and finish by painting it black. Finish with recessed joints using a piece of square sectioned wood about $\frac{3}{8} \times \frac{1}{4}″$ (1cm × 6mm) to shape them.

Fig. 2

Fig. 3

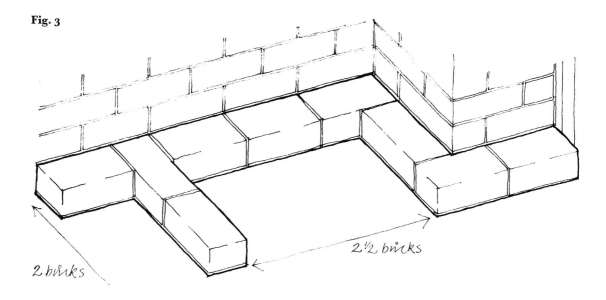

2½ bricks

2 bricks

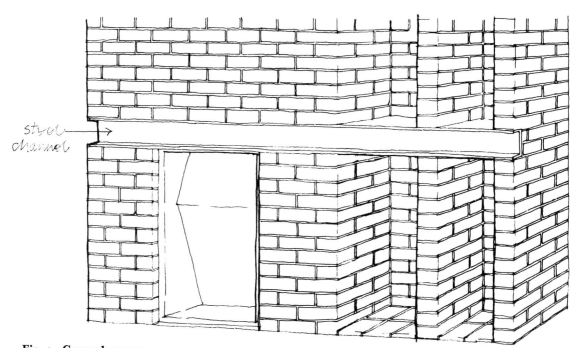

steel channel

Fig. 4 General arrangement

The hearth

Spread ½″ (1.2cm) of mortar over an area of about 3′ (90cm) and lay out a cord along the front edge as a guide. The actual length and width will vary in individual cases.

Set the quarry tiles or paving bricks on the mortar bed tapping them gently to set firmly, leaving a joint width of ¼″ (6mm). You can use strips of wood ¼″ (6mm) wide as spacers to ensure that the joints are constant. use the spirit level to make sure that your hearth is level.

Fill the joints with a neat cement grout, that is, cement mixed with water to a thick creamy consistency. Clean off the grout from the surface of the bricks with clean water and a cloth frequently rinsed out. Finally, a coat of linseed oil will give the paving bricks an attractive sheen.

Shelving

All there is left to do now is make the alcove shelves. Cut the blockboard to the size needed to fill the alcove spaces and cover the top with melamine laminate or use polished wood if you prefer. Plug and screw a $1'' \times 2''$ (2.5×2.5cm) wooden batten to the wall at the back of each alcove to carry the back edge of each shelf. This must be level with the top of the angle bearer on the steel channel. Screw each shelf from underneath. Complete the whole project by painting the steel channel. The colour of the bricks will determine the colour of paint but if you are unsure, black or very dark brown will be the best choice. Use a paint with an eggshell finish rather than a high gloss.

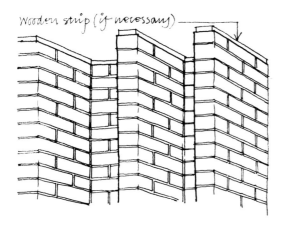

Fig. 5   Detail of ceiling junction

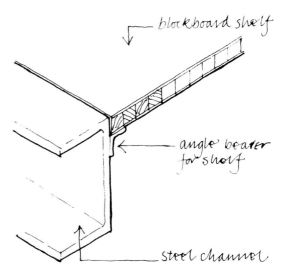

Fig. 6   Detail of shelf and channel

Sculpture

At first, the idea of a sculptor using common brick seems a difficult one to grasp. We are so used to seeing brick in its functional role that to consider it a material to be moulded or chiselled like stone or marble into creative forms, independent of any function, seems to present a problem. We can concede without too much trouble that brick walls look better embellished by decorative tricks like coloured mortar joints or header courses arranged in geometric patterns, but to pretend that a column of brick is the same as a noble uncut block of stone or marble seems to debase the very art of sculpture.

In fact, brick lends itself splendidly to the sculptor's chisel and the art of brick sculpture has a long pedigree. In the ancient worlds of Egypt and Greece, stone for quarrying was freely available, but further east, in the valley of the Euphrates and Tigris, the Babylonians and Assyrians had to make do with baked earth for their monuments. They found brick could be carved, moulded and coloured with ease and by 500 BC, the technique had attained great heights of sophistication: the Ishtar Gate at the north entrance to the city of Babylon glowed with coloured, glazed bricks on which were depicted yellow and white bulls and winged beasts in relief. Equally the Persians at Susa and Persepolis under Darius I built impressive palace complexes where each individual building was decorated with glazed bricks portraying processions of archers, lions, bulls or griffins (see also page 14).

Some two hundred years later in China, brick sculpture was produced by means of impressing the clay into stone or wooden moulds or by stamping it with blocks into various shapes, such as horses, chariots, trees and birds, for the decoration of burial chambers.

In northern Europe decorating brickwork had been a craft for hundreds of years and by 1510 in England carved brickwork was developing along-

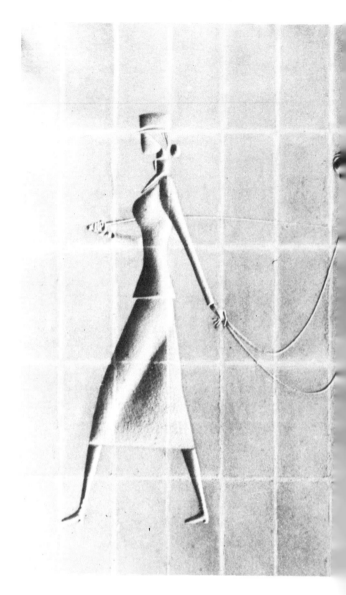

A Lady Returns from Dressage. *Shallow intaglio carving in white calcium silicate bricks by Walter Ritchie.*

side the art of terra-cotta modelling; the use of soft bricks of superior quality called 'rubbers' (because they could be rubbed into any chosen shape) became increasingly popular for decorating architectural details like arches, niches, columns and friezes. Examples of work in rubbers have come down to us from the late 17th century showing virtually no ill effects from weathering over the years.

The use of rubbed brickwork continued in Victorian times, but until recently was the province of the 'trade carver' or stone mason. In the 20s and 30s of our own century several sculptors emerged who preferred working with brick to any other material; they used rubbers set into a panel on buildings, or carved directly onto the brick.

Like other forms of sculpture, carving in brick can be made 'in the round' or 'in relief' by carving with special tools. 'Relief' is the projection or recession of a design from a flat surface where the flat surface is retained as an integral part of the composition. It may be incised or cut into the surface and in this case is called 'intaglio'. Pro-

jected relief falls into two major categories: firstly low relief in which the projection is slight—an effect like drawing on the carving surface; secondly high relief which is attained by using the complete form in the round projected, but at the same time keeping it attached to the background. Completely in the round, the sculpture becomes a three-dimensional solid object.

Throughout this book we have stressed the effectiveness of designing forms which can become 'sculptural' features of any area—a garden or patio for example—making it a more exciting place to live and rest in. We have been keen to engender a feel for the material itself; an eye for

dramatic shapes and sharp details and a love of
form for its own sake, whether it be in simple
tables, planters or grander structures like summer
houses and pergolas.

In this chapter we have included some illustrations of recent brick sculpture to inspire you to
try your hand and to think of brick as an artistic
material. The free-standing planter opposite is
rather more than a useful object for growing
plants, and has a presence that suggests that the
material from which it was made was thought
about in a creative way. Its sculptured contours
are achieved with normal bricks and a great deal of
skilful cutting. Its construction would involve
working out the proportions on paper and a
preliminary rough sketch.

Architects are generally feeling the desire to
break up large areas of brick walling with bold
relief decoration. As an example of this we have
included a picture of abstract shapes designed by
the famous sculptor Henry Moore and worked by
two master masons from plaster moulds: it certainly involved the close co-operation of the
craftsman and sculptor.

In the U.S. recently some interesting work has
been done. We have included here the piece
entitled *Equivalent VIII*, a sculpture comprising 120
fire bricks executed by the American artist Carl
André. When André's work crossed the Atlantic to
become part of the collection of the Tate Gallery in
London in 1976, it sparked off such a controversy
that the Brick Development Association was
moved to put on an exhibition of the work of
Walter Ritchie in the London Building Centre to
show the public another, less contentious, face of
contemporary brick sculpture —one that bears the
mark of a more traditional feel for the material.

These illustrations of Ritchie's work go only a
short way towards showing the range of his work;
from the first single brick he ever carved in 1953
(page 176) to one of his latest works 'The Lovers'
(page 177 and 179); which is one of a group of
seven pieces. His commissions span many countries: the U.S.A., Argentina, Germany, Switzer-
land as well as Great Britain.

Today he is probably England's best exponent
of the art and in a recent article in 'The Brick

*Free-standing planter of monumental proportions
dominates an urban landscape.*

Above: Equivalent VIII. *A sculpture comprising 120 fire bricks by Carl André.*

Left: Relief work designed by Henry Moore, originally for bronze and carved by master masons— Bouwcentrum, Rotterdam, Holland.

Bulletin' he describes his carving techniques, his method, and his preferences. On the subject of the sort of bricks he prefers when carving a wall, he says 'engineering bricks are too brittle to work but semi-engineering bricks are possible. The milder facings can be a pleasure to cut and take detail as well as a fine-grained limestone . . . Incised line carving, lettering or shallow concave designs are possible in practically any flush pointed wall of reasonable bricks, but carving proper, perhaps 3″ deep, needs plain bricks without frogs or perforations, laid and backed up solid. They should be damped before laying and bedded and struck in one operation . . . Mortar should be only slightly softer and more porous than the bricks to allow the outward movement of moisture and salts.'

His method consists of preparing a preliminary sketch which is transferred and reworked in full size onto his studio wall; he then photographs this and uses it as his reference while working on the wall to be carved.

The tools he uses include a sharp punch for

roughing out and a claw tool and flat tungsten tipped chisels for refining forms. He says: 'rasps, rifflers and bits of silicon carbide cuttings discs all have their uses but power tools have not proved necessary or desirable!'

Although there is no substitute for skill and talent, brick sculpture could be tried by the amateur without too much expense in his own home on inside or outside walls or a monolithic slab specially built for the purpose. Sharp tools, a feel for the material, an inspiration of an image, and confidence are what you need. You could begin with something quite small–using a single brick and carving an abstract, linear shape.

Suitable bricks

Most of the clay facing bricks are suitable for carving and if you are intending to construct a single slab for the purpose, it is best to build it from the softer facings with regular flush joints. If the carving block is an existing wall you have little choice, but choose an area where the brickwork is of even texture.

The grid of mortar joints can be emphasized or reduced but a bold treatment of both bonding pattern and joints can give a certain pleasure when seen from a distance with the grid showing up clearly (see *A Lady Returns from Dressage* on pages 170-71).

Calcium silicate bricks have a denser, granular feel and their softness makes them ideal for cutting. They have a natural white colour but most brickmakers sell a coloured range of the same brick.

We have already discussed coloured cements for jointing effects (page 23) and don't forget this when you are considering the colour and effect required for your sculpture. Today there are very new kinds of mortar mixes available containing adhesives (expoxy resins) for high bonding performance which allow large columns of thin brickwork to be built up and carved, even horizontally, without damage occurring to the joints even when unsupported in the centre. This is very new, so consult the experts for advice.

Even a single brick can be carved to great effect like the example of Walter Ritchie's here.

Be careful when carving a single brick as bricks without mortar joints to add strength are very fragile.

Above: Single brick carved in low relief by Walter Ritchie in 1953.

Right: Embracing Lovers: *carved by Walter Ritchie in low relief on red wirecut bricks.*

Tools

The tools to use for carving brick are the basic stone-carving tools which include three types of chisel, each with a different end, designed for the three stages of carving. They are known as the point, claw and flat chisel and as they are the most important tools, we describe their particular functions below.

In addition a hammer, called a dummy mallet, is required for hitting the chisels, a rasp for smoothing surfaces and a riffler (a tool with curved file surfaces) for filing parts that are difficult to reach. A sharpening stone will be needed to sharpen the chisels.

The point is used for the preliminary rough shaping of the sculpture. There are several types of point and when carving soft material like brick, the broader point or 'punch' is often used.

The point should be held firmly, blows with the hammer will remove lumps cleanly and it should be held at an angle of 45° to the surface which will allow the pieces to break cleanly away.

The claw is a tooth-edged implement used for the second stage of carving or where large areas are to be hollowed out as in intaglio. Using the claw leaves the surface covered with fine lines (look closely at the background detail of *The Lovers*). Claws come in a variety of widths.

The flat chisel is used for the final stage of carving and leaves the sculpture with a fairly smooth surface. When the shaping is completed, use it to finish the surface of the brick.

Lighting

When you have finished your sculpture, consider what lighting to use to show it off to best advantage. Some sculpture techniques benefit from a strong light coming from one direction. Intaglio relief looks better like this but others should be lit with a strong light from in front. If your first attempt at sculpture has not been a great success, dim lighting might be the best alternative!

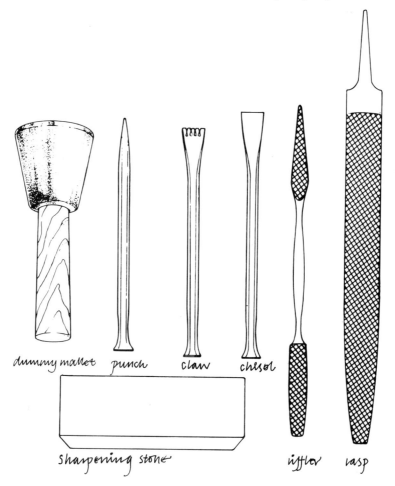

dummy mallet   punch   claw   chisel

sharpening stone

riffler   rasp

Detail of Embracing Lovers.

Estimating tables

Bricks
Use these guidelines when ordering bricks.
For 1 sq yd brickwork ½ brick thick you will need 48 bricks and 0.021 cu yds mortar.
For 1 sq yd brickwork 1 brick thick you will need 96 bricks and 0.042 cu yds mortar

For 1m brickwork ½ brick thick you will need 54 bricks and 0.024 m³ mortar.
For 1m brickwork 1 brick thick you will need 108 bricks and 0.048m³ mortar.

Note: These quantities are approximate and relate to a brick size nominally $4\frac{1}{2}'' \times 3'' \times 9''$. Other sizes will require adjustment. For example, a brick nominally $4'' \times 2\frac{2}{3}'' \times 8''$ with a $\frac{3}{8}''$ mortar joint will require roughly 20% more bricks for the same area of brickwork. The quantities do not allow for cutting and waste, so you must increase the amounts by 10% for ordering purposes.

Mortar
The proportions of a mortar or concrete mix relate to volume not weight. To enable you to measure the correct amounts into the mix, it is a good idea to make a box big enough to hold a certain volume of dry ingredients: a cubic foot would be a useful volume. Make a box 1 foot long × 1 foot high × 1 foot deep. Using this box, a 1:1:6 mortar mix will need 1 box of cement, one box of lime and 6 boxes of sand.

Ingredients for mortar mix 1:1:6
*Portland Cement comes in large sacks. The amount a sack contains varies from country to country. For instance in Great Britain a sack holds 112lbs (50 kilos) and in the U.S. 94 lbs.

Volume of mortar	Cement*	Lime	Sand
1 cu yd	448 lbs	224 lbs	1 cu yd
½ cu yd	224 lbs	112 lbs	½ cu yd
1 cu ft	16½ lbs	8¼ lbs	1 cu ft

Volume of mortar	Cement*	Lime	Sand
1m³	260 kilos	130 kilos	1m³
½m³	130 kilos	65 kilos	½m³
10dm³	2.6 kilos	1.3 kilos	10dm³

Note: In any project where a 1:1:6 and a 1:3 mortar mix is required, it will not be necessary to calculate two separate amounts. For estimating purposes, it will be reasonable to ignore the 1:3 mix as this will be quite a small amount, and estimate as if a 1:1:6 mix will be used throughout. Also, these quantities refer to bricks without perforations or frogs: for bricks with perforations or frogs, add 10%.

1 cu yd of mortar is sufficient to lay 2000 bricks
1 cu ft of mortar is sufficient to lay 74 bricks
1m³ of mortar is sufficient to lay 2600 bricks
10dm³ of mortar is sufficient to lay 26 bricks

Concrete
Ingredients for concrete mix 1:2:4

Volume of concrete	Cement	Sand	Aggregate	Water
1 cu yd	448 lbs	0.43 cu yds	0.86 cu yds	24 gall (approx)
½ cu yd	224 lbs	0.21 cu yds	0.43 cu yds	12 gall (approx)

Volume of concrete	Cement	Sand	Aggregate	Water
1m³	258 kilos	0.56m³	1m³	245 lit
½m³	129 kilos	0.28m³	0.5m³	122 lit

1 cu yd (m³) of concrete will cover:
12 sq yds (15m²) 3″ (7.5cm) thick
9 sq yds (10m²) 4″ (10cm) thick
6 sq yds (7.5m²) 6″ (15cm) thick

Useful information

SIZES OF AMERICAN MODULAR BRICK

Name	Nominal Dimensions, in.			Joint Thickness in.	Manufactured Dimensions in.			Modular Coursing in.
	t	h	l		t	h	l	
Standard Modular	4	$2\frac{2}{3}$	8	$\frac{3}{8}$	$3\frac{5}{8}$	$2\frac{1}{4}$	$7\frac{5}{8}$	$3C = 8$
				$\frac{1}{2}$	$3\frac{1}{2}$	$2\frac{1}{4}$	$7\frac{1}{2}$	
Engineer	4	$3\frac{1}{5}$	8	$\frac{3}{8}$	$3\frac{5}{8}$	$2\frac{13}{16}$	$7\frac{5}{8}$	$5C = 16$
				$\frac{1}{2}$	$3\frac{1}{2}$	$2\frac{11}{16}$	$7\frac{1}{2}$	
Economy 8 or Jumbo Closure	4	4	8	$\frac{3}{8}$	$3\frac{5}{8}$	$3\frac{5}{8}$	$7\frac{5}{8}$	$1C = 4$
				$\frac{1}{2}$	$3\frac{1}{2}$	$3\frac{1}{2}$	$7\frac{1}{2}$	
Double	4	$5\frac{1}{3}$	8	$\frac{3}{8}$	$3\frac{5}{8}$	$4\frac{15}{16}$	$7\frac{5}{8}$	$3C = 16$
				$\frac{1}{2}$	$3\frac{1}{2}$	$4\frac{13}{16}$	$7\frac{1}{2}$	
Roman	4	2	12	$\frac{3}{8}$	$3\frac{5}{8}$	$1\frac{5}{8}$	$11\frac{5}{8}$	$2C = 4$
				$\frac{1}{2}$	$3\frac{1}{2}$	$1\frac{1}{2}$	$11\frac{1}{2}$	
Norman	4	$2\frac{2}{3}$	12	$\frac{3}{8}$	$3\frac{5}{8}$	$2\frac{1}{4}$	$11\frac{5}{8}$	$3C = 8$
				$\frac{1}{2}$	$3\frac{1}{2}$	$2\frac{1}{4}$	$11\frac{1}{2}$	
Norwegian	4	$3\frac{1}{5}$	12	$\frac{3}{8}$	$3\frac{5}{8}$	$2\frac{13}{16}$	$11\frac{5}{8}$	$5C = 16$
				$\frac{1}{2}$	$3\frac{1}{2}$	$2\frac{11}{16}$	$11\frac{1}{2}$	
Economy 12 or Jumbo Utility	4	4	12	$\frac{3}{8}$	$3\frac{5}{8}$	$3\frac{5}{8}$	$11\frac{5}{8}$	$1C = 4$
				$\frac{1}{2}$	$3\frac{1}{2}$	$3\frac{1}{2}$	$11\frac{1}{2}$	
Triple	4	$5\frac{1}{3}$	12	$\frac{3}{8}$	$3\frac{5}{8}$	$4\frac{15}{16}$	$11\frac{5}{8}$	$3C = 16$
				$\frac{1}{2}$	$3\frac{1}{2}$	$4\frac{13}{16}$	$11\frac{1}{2}$	
SCR brick	6	$2\frac{2}{3}$	12	$\frac{3}{8}$	$5\frac{5}{8}$	$2\frac{1}{4}$	$11\frac{5}{8}$	$3C = 8$
				$\frac{1}{2}$	$5\frac{1}{2}$	$2\frac{1}{4}$	$11\frac{1}{2}$	
6-in. Norwegian	6	$3\frac{1}{5}$	12	$\frac{3}{8}$	$5\frac{5}{8}$	$2\frac{13}{16}$	$11\frac{5}{8}$	$5C = 16$
				$\frac{1}{2}$	$5\frac{1}{2}$	$2\frac{11}{16}$	$11\frac{1}{2}$	
6-in. Jumbo	6	4	12	$\frac{3}{8}$	$5\frac{5}{8}$	$3\frac{5}{8}$	$11\frac{5}{8}$	$1C = 4$
				$\frac{1}{2}$	$5\frac{1}{2}$	$3\frac{1}{2}$	$11\frac{1}{2}$	
8-in. Jumbo	8	4	12	$\frac{3}{8}$	$7\frac{5}{8}$	$3\frac{5}{8}$	$11\frac{5}{8}$	$1C = 4$
				$\frac{1}{2}$	$7\frac{1}{2}$	$3\frac{1}{2}$	$11\frac{1}{2}$	

This table is reproduced by kind permission of the Brick Institute of America

VERTICAL COURSING TABLE FOR AMERICAN MODULAR BRICK

No. of Courses	Nominal Height (h) of Unit				
	$2''$	$2\frac{2}{3}''$	$3\frac{1}{5}''$	$4''$	$5\frac{1}{3}''$
1	$2''$	$2\frac{11}{16}''$	$3\frac{3}{16}''$	$4''$	$5\frac{5}{16}''$
2	$4''$	$5\frac{5}{16}''$	$6\frac{3}{8}''$	$8''$	$10\frac{11}{16}''$
3	$6''$	$8''$	$9\frac{5}{8}''$	$1'\ 0''$	$1'\ 4''$
4	$8''$	$10\frac{11}{16}''$	$1'\ 0\frac{3}{16}''$	$1'\ 4''$	$1'\ 9\frac{5}{16}''$
5	$10''$	$1'\ 1\frac{5}{16}''$	$1'\ 4''$	$1'\ 8''$	$2'\ 2\frac{11}{16}''$
6	$1'\ 0''$	$1'\ 4''$	$1'\ 7\frac{3}{16}''$	$2'\ 0''$	$2'\ 8''$
7	$1'\ 2''$	$1'\ 6\frac{11}{16}''$	$1'\ 10\frac{3}{8}''$	$2'\ 4''$	$3'\ 1\frac{5}{16}''$
8	$1'\ 4''$	$1'\ 9\frac{5}{16}''$	$2'\ 1\frac{5}{8}''$	$2'\ 8''$	$3'\ 6\frac{11}{16}''$
9	$1'\ 6''$	$2'\ 0''$	$2'\ 4\frac{13}{16}''$	$3'\ 0''$	$4'\ 0''$
10	$1'\ 8''$	$2'\ 2\frac{11}{16}''$	$2'\ 8''$	$3'\ 4''$	$4'\ 5\frac{5}{16}''$
11	$1'\ 10''$	$2'\ 5\frac{5}{16}''$	$2'\ 11\frac{3}{16}''$	$3'\ 8''$	$4'\ 10\frac{11}{16}''$
12	$2'\ 0''$	$2'\ 8''$	$3'\ 2\frac{3}{8}''$	$4'\ 0''$	$5'\ 4''$
13	$2'\ 2''$	$2'\ 10\frac{11}{16}''$	$3'\ 5\frac{5}{8}''$	$4'\ 4''$	$5'\ 9\frac{5}{16}''$
14	$2'\ 4''$	$3'\ 1\frac{5}{16}''$	$3'\ 8\frac{13}{16}''$	$4'\ 8''$	$6'\ 2\frac{11}{16}''$
15	$2'\ 6''$	$3'\ 4''$	$4'\ 0''$	$5'\ 0''$	$6'\ 8''$
16	$2'\ 8''$	$3'\ 6\frac{11}{16}''$	$4'\ 3\frac{3}{16}''$	$5'\ 4''$	$7'\ 1\frac{5}{16}''$
17	$2'\ 10''$	$3'\ 9\frac{5}{16}''$	$4'\ 6\frac{3}{8}''$	$5'\ 8''$	$7'\ 6\frac{11}{16}''$
18	$3'\ 0''$	$4'\ 0''$	$4'\ 9\frac{5}{8}''$	$6'\ 0''$	$8'\ 0''$
19	$3'\ 2''$	$4'\ 2\frac{11}{16}''$	$5'\ 0\frac{13}{16}''$	$6'\ 4''$	$8'\ 5\frac{5}{16}''$
20	$3'\ 4''$	$4'\ 5\frac{5}{16}''$	$5'\ 4''$	$6'\ 8''$	$8'\ 10\frac{11}{16}''$
21	$3'\ 6''$	$4'\ 8''$	$5'\ 7\frac{3}{16}''$	$7'\ 0''$	$9'\ 4''$
22	$3'\ 8''$	$4'\ 10\frac{11}{16}''$	$5'\ 10\frac{3}{8}''$	$7'\ 4''$	$9'\ 9\frac{5}{16}''$
23	$3'\ 10''$	$5'\ 1\frac{5}{16}''$	$6'\ 1\frac{5}{8}''$	$7'\ 8''$	$10'\ 2\frac{11}{16}''$
24	$4'\ 0''$	$5'\ 4''$	$6'\ 4\frac{13}{16}''$	$8'\ 0''$	$10'\ 8''$
25	$4'\ 2''$	$5'\ 6\frac{11}{16}''$	$6'\ 8''$	$8'\ 4''$	$11'\ 1\frac{5}{16}''$
26	$4'\ 4''$	$5'\ 9\frac{5}{16}''$	$6'\ 11\frac{3}{16}''$	$8'\ 8''$	$11'\ 6\frac{11}{16}''$
27	$4'\ 6''$	$6'\ 0''$	$7'\ 2\frac{3}{8}''$	$9'\ 0''$	$12'\ 0''$
28	$4'\ 8''$	$6'\ 2\frac{11}{16}''$	$7'\ 5\frac{5}{8}''$	$9'\ 4''$	$12'\ 5\frac{5}{16}''$
29	$4'\ 10''$	$6'\ 5\frac{5}{16}''$	$7'\ 8\frac{13}{16}''$	$9'\ 8''$	$12'\ 10\frac{11}{16}''$
30	$5'\ 0''$	$6'\ 8''$	$8'\ 0''$	$10'\ 0''$	$13'\ 4''$
31	$5'\ 2''$	$6'\ 10\frac{11}{16}''$	$8'\ 3\frac{3}{16}''$	$10'\ 4''$	$13'\ 9\frac{5}{16}''$
32	$5'\ 4''$	$7'\ 1\frac{5}{16}''$	$8'\ 6\frac{3}{8}''$	$10'\ 8''$	$14'\ 2\frac{11}{16}''$
33	$5'\ 6''$	$7'\ 4''$	$8'\ 9\frac{5}{8}''$	$11'\ 0''$	$14'\ 8''$
34	$5'\ 8''$	$7'\ 6\frac{11}{16}''$	$9'\ 0\frac{13}{16}''$	$11'\ 4''$	$15'\ 1\frac{5}{16}''$
35	$5'\ 10''$	$7'\ 9\frac{5}{16}''$	$9'\ 4''$	$11'\ 8''$	$15'\ 6\frac{11}{16}''$
36	$6'\ 0''$	$8'\ 0''$	$9'\ 7\frac{3}{16}''$	$12'\ 0''$	$16'\ 0''$
37	$6'\ 2''$	$8'\ 2\frac{11}{16}''$	$9'\ 10\frac{3}{8}''$	$12'\ 4''$	$16'\ 5\frac{5}{16}''$
38	$6'\ 4''$	$8'\ 5\frac{5}{16}''$	$10'\ 1\frac{5}{8}''$	$12'\ 8''$	$16'\ 10\frac{11}{16}''$
39	$6'\ 6''$	$8'\ 8''$	$10'\ 4\frac{13}{16}''$	$13'\ 0''$	$17'\ 4''$
40	$6'\ 8''$	$8'\ 10\frac{11}{16}''$	$10'\ 8''$	$13'\ 4''$	$17'\ 9\frac{5}{16}''$
41	$6'\ 10''$	$9'\ 1\frac{5}{16}''$	$10'\ 11\frac{3}{16}''$	$13'\ 8''$	$18'\ 2\frac{11}{16}''$
42	$7'\ 0''$	$9'\ 4''$	$11'\ 2\frac{3}{8}''$	$14'\ 0''$	$18'\ 8''$
43	$7'\ 2''$	$9'\ 6\frac{11}{16}''$	$11'\ 5\frac{5}{8}''$	$14'\ 4''$	$19'\ 1\frac{5}{16}''$
44	$7'\ 4''$	$9'\ 9\frac{5}{16}''$	$11'\ 8\frac{13}{16}''$	$14'\ 8''$	$19'\ 6\frac{11}{16}''$
45	$7'\ 6''$	$10'\ 0''$	$12'\ 0''$	$15'\ 0''$	$20'\ 0''$
46	$7'\ 8''$	$10'\ 2\frac{11}{16}''$	$12'\ 3\frac{3}{16}''$	$15'\ 4''$	$20'\ 5\frac{5}{16}''$
47	$7'\ 10''$	$10'\ 5\frac{5}{16}''$	$12'\ 6\frac{3}{8}''$	$15'\ 8''$	$20'\ 10\frac{11}{16}''$
48	$8'\ 0''$	$10'\ 8''$	$12'\ 9\frac{5}{8}''$	$16'\ 0''$	$21'\ 4''$
49	$8'\ 2''$	$10'\ 10\frac{11}{16}''$	$13'\ 0\frac{13}{16}''$	$16'\ 4''$	$21'\ 9\frac{5}{16}''$
50	$8'\ 4''$	$11'\ 1\frac{5}{16}''$	$13'\ 4''$	$16'\ 8''$	$22'\ 2\frac{11}{16}''$

Note: For convenience in using the table, nominal $\frac{1}{3}''$, $\frac{2}{3}''$ and $\frac{1}{5}''$ heights of units have been changed to the nearest $\frac{1}{16}''$. Vertical dimensions are from bottom of mortar joint to bottom of mortar joint.

This table is reproduced by kind permission of the Brick Institute of America.

A modern brick fireplace with the chimney breast supported by a flat arch and lintel.

Useful addresses

The Brick Institute of America
1750 Old Meadow Road
McLean
Virginia 22101
U.S.A.

The Brick Development Association
19 Grafton Street
London WC1

The Brick Advisory Centre
26 Store Street
London WC1

The Brick Manufacturers Association
44A Railway Parade
Burwood
New South Wales
2134 Australia

Glossary

ABSORPTION The weight of water a brick or tile will absorb when immersed in either cold or boiling water for a stated length of time.

AGGREGATE Broken gravel, stone, slag or sand used with cement to form concrete. Aggregate can be coarse or fine, and is measured by the size of mesh through which it is passed.

ARCH A curved structural member which spans openings or recesses.

BALLAST Excavated material from sea or river deposits and used as an aggregate in concrete.

BAT A piece of brick referred to by size, e.g. half bat or quarter bat.

BED A bearing surface of any component in a building at right angles to the loading pressure.

BED-DEPTH The thickness of a brick as opposed to height or length.

BLOCKBOARD A built-up board with a core of wooden strips laid with alternating grain and glued between outer veneers whose grains run in the opposite direction.

BRICK A solid masonry unit of clay or shale made in a rectangular prism and fired in a kiln.

Common or Building Brick Brick for building purposes and not treated or textured for colour.

Facing Brick Brick treated to produce surface texture, made in selected clays to create desired colour.

Fire Brick Brick made with refractory ceramic material and resistant to very high termperatures.

Paving Brick Vitrified brick, suitable for paving.

Soft Mud Brick Brick made by moulding wet clay by a hand process.

Stiff Mud Brick Brick made by extruding a stiff but plastic clay through a die.

BUTTERING Putting mortar on a masonry unit with a trowel.

CAVITY WALL Wall constructed of two separate thicknessess, which are connected at intervals by wall ties.

CENTRING Temporary structure for support of arches and lintels during construction.

CLEAT A small piece of wood or metal used to fix two members.

CLOSER A brick cut to complete the bond at the end or corner of a wall. See also *Queen Closer*.

COPING A cap or finish on top of a wall, pier, chimney etc. serving to protect masonry below.

COUNTERSINKING The conical sinking round the end of a hole drilled for a screw, which allows the screw head to lie flush with the surrounding material.

COURSE A continuous horizontal layer bonded by mortar in masonry.

DAMP-PROOF COURSE A layer of impervious material, to prevent moisture from rising.

DRYWELL See *Soakaway*.

EFFLORESCENCE A powdery white stain on a wall surface and seen when the wall dries out, caused by deposition of water-soluble salts.

FACING Any material used for forming a finished surface.

FASCIA BOARD A wide board set vertically on edge and fixed to the lower ends of the rafters to the wall plate or the wall.

FIBREBOARD Made of felted wood and used for its insulation properties.

FLASHING A thin impervious material place over joints and air spaces to prevent water penetration and*or provide water drainage.

FLOAT A rectangular wooden tool used for smoothing plaster.

FORMWORK Temporary construction of wood within which concrete is cast.

FROG A depression in bed surface of brick. Sometimes known as a panel.

GALVANIZING Coating of zinc given to ferrous metal to provide protection from corrosion.

GAUGE ROD A marked pole for measuring masonry coursing during construction.

GRAVEL Collection of small rounded stones.

GROUT A cementitious component of high water cement ratio, allowing it to be poured into small spaces.

GULLEY A trap in which rain and waste water are collected before entering the drain.

GUTTER A channel placed along eaves of a roof or edge of a path for removal of rainwater.

HARDBURNT Fired at high temperature, and made of nearly vitrified clay. The products have a low absorption but a high compressive strength.

HALF BAT Brick cut in half width ways.

HARDBOARD Man-made board of wooden fibres felted and formed under pressure.

HARDCORE Broken bricks etc. used for foundations for paths, drives and solid concrete floors.

HAWK A square board with a short vertical handle beneath.

HEADER A brick laid so that the end shows on the face of the wall.

HOGGING Coarse sand, sifted gravel or fine ballast.

JOIST A wood or steel beam directly supporting a floor and sometimes alternatively or additionally supporting a ceiling.

LEAD The section of a wall built up and racked back on successive courses.

LINTEL A beam placed over an opening in a wall.

MASONRY Brick tile, stone etc. or combination, bonded with mortar.

MASONRY CEMENT A mill-mixed mortar to which sand and water must be added.

MITRE The intersection of two pieces of brick, wood etc. meeting at an angle. The line of the mitre bisects the angle and is 45° for a right-angled corner, so that corresponding shapes in a moulding meet on the mitre and turn the corner.

MORTAR A plastic mixture of cementitious materials, fine aggregate and water.

NICHE A recess in a wall.

NOMINAL DIMENSION In masonry, a dimension greater by the thickness of a mortar joint than specified.

PANEL PIN A slender wire nail with a small head, which is hardly seen when driven into the surface of joinery work.

PIER 1) An isolated column of masonry. 2) see also *Pilaster*.

PILASTER A wall portion projecting from either or both wall faces and serving as a vertical column and or beam.

PLYWOOD A board made from a number of sheets of veneer and glued together, the grain of adjacent sheets being at right-angles to each other.

POINTING Trowelling mortar into a joint after masonry units are laid.

QUEEN CLOSER A cut brick having a nominal horizontal face dimension.

QUOIN A projecting right angle masonry corner.

RETURN Any surface turned back from the face of the main surface.

REVEAL That portion of a jamb or recess which is visible from the face of a wall back to the frame placed between jambs.

RISER The upright face of a step.

ROWLOCK A brick laid on its face edge so that the normal bedding area is visible in the wall face. Also referred to as brick-on-edge.

RUBBER A soft brick which can be shaped by rubbing with an abrasive.

RUBBLE 1) Broken bricks, old plaster and similar waste material. 2) Stones of irregular size and shape used in walling

SCR Structural Clay Research (trademark of the Brick Institute of America).

SCREED A layer of mortar giving a smooth surface which will be suitable for floor tiles, linoleum etc.

SHOE A metal socket enclosing the end of a beam etc.

SKIN See *Wythe*

SLENDERNESS RATIO Ratio of the effective height of a member to its effective thickness.

SOAKAWAY A pit filled with broken stones etc. to take drainage from rainwater pipes or land drains and let it disperse. Also known as a drywell.

SOCKET 1) The enlarged end of a pipe into which another pipe is fitted. 2) A cavity into which anything is fitted.

SOFT-BURNT Fired at a low temperature producing high absorption but low compressive strength.

SOLDIER A stretcher set on end with face showing on the wall surface.

STORY POLE See *Gauge Rod*.

STRETCHER The long face of a brick.

STRUCK JOINT Any mortar joint which has been finished with a trowel.

TAMPING BOARD A board used for consolidating concrete within its forms and for levelling the concrete.

TEMPLATE A full size pattern usually made of wood or sheet metal and used as a testing shape when building.

TIE Any unit of material which connects masonry.

TOOLING Compressing and shaping the face of a mortar joint with a special tool other than a trowel.

WALL TIE A connection of wythes of masonry by a bonder or metal piece.

WEEP HOLES Openings which are placed in mortar joints of facing material to allow the escape of moisture.

WYTHE A continuous vertical section of masonry one unit in thickness.

Unusual brick paving in an urban setting.

Picture acknowledgements

Permission to reproduce photographs has kindly been given by the following:

Ronald Adam Associates: 19 (both), 23, 28, 36, 39, 43, 45 (both), 48, 55, 56, 71, 72-3, 75, 82, 101, 116, 123, 170-1, 172-3, 174-5, 177, 179, 182. Courtesy of the Architectural Association: 14, 44. Brecht-Einzig Limited: 6, 77 (bottom), 115. Brick Institute of America: 68-9. J. Allan Cash Ltd 127. Civic Trust: 58. Design Council: 187. Cecil C. Handisyde: 18, 42. Rosalined Howell: 17, 52, 76 (bottom), 119 (top left and right). Ibstock Building Products Limited: 70. Mary Evans Picture Library: 12, 13. The National Monuments Record: 16 (both), 22. The National Trust, Bodnant Garden: 76-7; Powis Castle: 119 (bottom). Walter Ritchie: 176. Ronald Sheridan: 15, 50-1. Stephenson Gibney & Associates, Architects and Industrial Designers, photograph by Tim Street-Porter: 66-7. Syndication International: 8, 74. The Tate Gallery: 175 (top).

The following photographs were specially taken for the book by Dawson Strange Photographers: 33: Phillip Griffiths: 40.

The following line drawings are by Stuart Perry: 24-5, 26, 27, 30, 34-5, 63, 65, 92, 178.

Index